Practical Handbooks

ire

Books are to be returned on
or before the last date shown

Learning and Teaching with Virtual Learning Environments

Learning and Teaching with Virtual Learning Environments

Helena Gillespie, Helen Boulton, Alison Hramiak and Richard Williamson

LearningMatters

First published in 2007 by Learning Matters Ltd

British Library Cataloguing in Publication Data
A CIP record for this book is available from the British Library.

ISBN: 978 1 84445 076 3

Cover design by Topics – The Creative Partnership
Project management by Deer Park Productions, Tavistock, Devon
Typeset by PDQ Typesetting Ltd
Printed and bound in Great Britain by Cromwell Press Ltd, Trowbridge, Wiltshire

Learning Matters Ltd
33 Southernhay East
Exeter EX1 1NX
Tel: 01392 215560
Email: info@learningmatters.co.uk
www.learningmatters.co.uk

Contents

The authors   vii

Acknowledgements   ix

1 Introduction   1

2 Teaching and learning using a VLE – blending face-to-face and online learning   7

3 Learning objects   20

4 Talk, chat and discussion – communications in virtual learning   36

5 Electronic portfolios – outcomes for virtual learning   49

6 Tasks, tests and feedback   62

7 Design issues – how to design virtual learning   75

8 Introducing a VLE into school   84

Appendix – Installing Moodle on a Windows Machine   97

Glossary   99

Index   101

The authors

Helena Gillespie (editor) teaches science, ICT and history on the Primary PGCE at the University of East Anglia in Norwich. She has taught for 10 years across the primary age range, specialising in working with pupils with special needs. She also worked as an ICT consultant to the LEA. Her research interests are in the field of the learning environment and VLEs and her research has been funded by the Training and Development Agency for Schools. She has written on the subject of ICT in schools and higher education for journals and in books.

Helen Boulton is a principal lecturer and strand leader for the PGCE (secondary) in ICT at Nottingham Trent University. In addition she is the learning and teaching co-ordinator for the School of Education. Prior to this she was an ICT co-ordinator for 10 years in a large secondary school, and also has extensive experience as an ICT co-ordinator in further education. Her research interests are in the field of e-learning and VLEs within secondary education.

Alison Hramiak is the course leader for the secondary PGCE in Applied ICT and also teaches on Masters in E-Learning at Sheffield Hallam University. She is the co-ordinator for, and teaches on, the general professional studies module which is taught to all subject PGCE students. Her research interests are in the field of the application of e-learning to teaching and learning, and the professional development of teachers, particularly through the use of VLEs within secondary education.

Richard Williamson is Head of ICT at Garibaldi College, a large 11–18 secondary school with specialist status in mathematics and computers. He is also e-learning co-ordinator, ICT PGCE and GTP mentor, ITT co-ordinator and part-time lecturer at Nottingham Trent University. Richard has pioneered the introduction of VLEs at a number of East Midlands schools, and has provided consultancy to LEAs regarding VLEs. He is currently studying for a Masters in Educational Leadership and Management.

Acknowledgements

As a team the authors would like to thank those who have made this book possible, the team at Learning Matters including Julia Morris and Jennifer Clark. We would also like to thank those who gave their permission for images of VLEs to be used, specifically Martin Dougiamas at Moodle and Dylan Jones at Netmedia. We would like to thank the Association for IT in Teacher Education (ITTE) for bringing us together as a team in the first place.

We also have some personal thanks to add.

Alison Hramiak would like to thank the mentors and teachers associated with the Applied ICT PGCE at Sheffield Hallam University for their ideas and examples. She would also particularly like to thank Karen Pole for her guidance and support and, at times, for just listening, throughout the writing of the chapters. Finally she would like to thank her fellow authors for the immense sprit of teamwork and friendship that has made this work tremendously enjoyable throughout.

Helen Boulton offers her enormous thanks to her parents and daughter, Holly, for their continued support and encouragement.

Helena Gillespie would like to thank her family for their support yet again, and would also like to thank all her friends, especially the 'virtual' ones for teaching her about life online. Finally, thanks to her fellow authors who made writing the book such good fun.

1
Introduction

Why you need this book

Information and communications technologies (ICTs) change fast. Year on year teachers are asked to take on new and innovative ideas from the world of ICT and use them to good effect in their teaching. One such innovation is virtual learning. This presents a significant challenge to teachers at all stages in their careers. This is because teachers need to learn how to work each new bit of technology and know when to use it. This book is designed to help with both things. For this reason it is suitable for teachers at all stages of their career development. However, it is particularly suitable for teachers undertaking their initial training because it sets the issues of virtual learning securely within the context of other teaching and learning issues such as planning, assessment and resourcing so it is easy to integrate virtual teaching and learning into developing classroom practice.

What is virtual learning?

'Virtual learning' is a term that has begun to be used in schools and education in general to describe an application that enables teachers and learners to do some or all of the following:

- share files;
- download information;
- email;
- use discussion boards;
- undertake tests and surveys;
- share information;
- organise time and resources;
- link teaching and learning applications and activities with management information systems.

This is usually done through an application that runs over an intranet or the internet and is viewed through a web browser such as Internet Explorer, Firefox or Safari. The tools to do the tasks listed (and in some cases others) are collected together as an application variously known as a virtual learning environment (VLE), managed learning environment (MLE) or learning platform (LP). The distinctions between these different kinds of virtual learning facilitators have become increasing blurred as functionality develops, and it is pointless to try to differentiate between them for the purposes of this book. We have chosen to call this application a virtual learning environment, but this does not mean that we are excluding from the discussion virtual learning tools known by the other names.

Virtual learning and the National Curriculum

Information and communications technology (ICT) is a subject in its own right in the National Curriculum (NC). This means that teachers must teach the skills and knowledge prescribed by the NC. The knowledge, skills and understanding come under four headings in each of the four key stages.

1. Finding things out.
2. Developing ideas and making things happen.
3. Exchanging and sharing information.
4. Reviewing, modifying and evaluating work as it progresses.

In addition, for each key stage the NC describes a 'breadth of study', which sets the contexts within which the knowledge, skills and understanding should be taught.

ICT is also referred to in the General Teaching Requirements element of the National Curriculum:

General teaching requirements

Use of information and communications technology across the curriculum

1. Pupils should be given opportunities to apply and develop their ICT capability through the use of ICT tools to support their learning in all subjects (at Key Stage 1, there are no statutory requirements to teach the use of ICT in the programmes of study for the non-core foundation subjects. Teachers should use their judgement to decide where it is appropriate to teach the use of ICT across these subjects at Key Stage 1. At other key stages, there are statutory requirements to use ICT in all subjects, except physical education).

2. Pupils should be given opportunities to support their work by being taught to:
a) find things out from a variety of sources, selecting and synthesising the information to meet their needs and developing an ability to question its accuracy, bias and plausibility;
b) develop their ideas using ICT tools to amend and refine their work and enhance its quality and accuracy;
c) exchange and share information, both directly and through electronic media;
d) review, modify and evaluate their work, reflecting critically on its quality, as it progresses.

Those planning for the curriculum often overlook these general teaching requirements, but they are highly pertinent in the context of virtual learning. This is not to say that in using a VLE elements of the subject-based NC would not be covered; indeed many elements of ICT and other subjects could be effectively taught, as this book will demonstrate. However, teaching and learning using a VLE enable schools and teachers to meet the general requirements effectively and in a meaningful way. Some examples, which can be matched to the general teaching requirements as outlined above, could include the following.

- **A VLE can give opportunities for pupils to apply their ICT knowledge skills and understanding in a useful context.**
- **A VLE can offer pupils a range of sources of information for their studies which can be selected and organised by their teachers in order to ensure that the resources are relevant to the learning.**
- **A VLE enables pupils to create and store digital work which can refined as a project progresses.**
- **A VLE enables pupils and teachers to communicate and collaborate in a number of ways.**

The NC and associated schemes and strategies develop and change rapidly. While, at the time of writing, there is no specific requirement to use a VLE as prescribed by the NC, a VLE enables teachers to meet the requirements of the NC very effectively.

Virtual learning and the future of schools

When VLEs first began to develop in the late 1990s, they were a combination of communications tools and file-sharing applications. These were often 'home-grown' solutions developed by educational establishments. Since then VLEs have become increasingly important (BECTa, 2003) and more and more research has been undertaken into the educational possibilities of virtual learning. This has also led to the rise of the term 'blended learning' where virtual and face-to-face learning are combined. For the majority of pupils in schools this will be their experience of virtual learning – as a complement to existing face-to-face teaching strategies. In some fields of education, especially in higher education, VLEs are being used as the sole tool for delivering courses to students, although of course the concept of distance learning in higher education is nothing new.

However, in the compulsory schooling sector, in both primary schools and secondary schools, virtual learning looks set to be a significant tool in enhancing teaching and learning, but it will not replace the traditional interface of teachers and pupils in classrooms. The possibilities of virtual learning are considered generally to be worth pursuing and to this end there is a requirement that by 2008 all schools will be using a learning platform of some kind. This puts significant pressure on existing ICT systems in schools to have the capacity and bandwidth to cope with such a system. More importantly, teachers must develop their teaching skills in order to make best use of the new possibilities for creative and good quality teaching and learning which virtual learning offers. Historically, ICT developments in schools have been hampered by inappropriate in-service training, and although generally speaking trainee teachers are well served by the ICT aspects their initial teacher training, their skills quickly date. It is very important for all teachers, both those beginning their careers and those already in post, to develop their skills in using virtual learning in their teaching. We hope that this book will be helpful in this.

The impact of virtual learning on teachers' professional development

There are two main areas of professional development needed if virtual learning is to be effective in schools. Firstly, teachers need to develop the technical skills needed to use a virtual learning environment. In essence these skills are not specific to using a particular VLE but they are general ICT skills, which can be transferred between learning platforms. However, it is not enough just to know the technical skills: as a teacher you also need to develop the appropriate pedagogical skills. So in addition you need to learn strategies to include virtual learning in your teaching and learning plans, both in the context of a long-term plan and at the lesson-planning level. Below is a list of some of the technical and pedagogical skills that you need to develop as a teacher in order to use virtual learning effectively.

Technical skills:

- **web browser navigation;**
- **making and uploading files of content (text, images, videos, MP3, etc.);**
- **adding and organising virtual learning tools;**
- **setting up discussion boards and other communications tools;**
- **constructing quizzes, surveys and tests;**
- **managing users of the VLE.**

Pedagogical skills:

- **organising the introduction of the VLE to learners;**
- **planning virtual learning opportunities in face-to-face teaching sessions;**
- **using virtual learning to develop non-classroom based learning opportunities;**
- **choosing and using appropriate content and communications tools;**
- **making the most of online learning opportunities.**

Clearly these two sets of skills cannot be learned in isolation and programmes of professional development need to include both of these aspects to be effective. This book is not designed to be a 'teach-yourself VLE' guide. Each of the learning platforms requires the application of technical skills in a particular way, and that cannot be covered in a book like this. Therefore we have focused our attention on the pedagogical skills. If you want to use this book as a self-study guide we suggest that you download help sheets from the VLE you are working with. These combined with the advice and support given in this book will help you develop effective skills in teaching and learning using a virtual learning environment.

In the book we do not endorse a particular VLE or learning platform: all the solutions, whether home-grown, open source or commercial, have things to recommend them.

How to use this book

This book is primarily designed with trainee and beginning teachers in mind, but can also be used by more experienced teachers. The specific nature of your teaching responsibilities will determine how you use this book, but we can offer some general advice.

- *Start with a small-scale virtual learning project* – look at Chapter 2 on blended learning for ways to integrate virtual learning projects into your face-to-face teaching.
- *Consider how you will develop your own skills as you progress* – Chapter 3 lists and describes all the different types of tools you may encounter in a VLE. Choose the ones which are most important and relevant in your situation and use these first, planning to include others once you are secure in your understanding of the most important tools.
- *Evaluate the effectiveness of the project* – Chapter 7 on design issues discusses how to plan and develop a VLE. Setting goals and targets at the design stage should help you evaluate your work as you go along.
- *Use the functionality of a VLE to make learning for your pupils challenging and exciting* – Chapters 4 and 5 respectively tackle communications and electronic portfolios. Both of these uses of virtual learning have the potential to be inspirational to your learners. Well-motivated learners will make your hard work in learning to use the VLE worthwhile.
- *Work with colleagues if you can* – Chapter 8 deals with the implementation of a VLE in a school. Whether you are working towards whole-school implementation or experimenting with virtual learning in your own context, considering the technical and practical issues in collaboration with colleagues is a critical success factor to the success of the project.
- *Look upon virtual learning as just one aspect of your continuing professional development* – learning virtual teaching skills has many links and parallels with face-to-face traditional teaching skills. It makes most sense to develop your understanding of teaching and learning in both situations together. A good example of this would be to develop ideas about assessing pupils' learning in traditional ways alongside developing ideas about how to do this using a VLE. Chapter 6 deals with some of these issues.

Features of this book

This book is not designed to be read cover to cover. We hope that the layout will help you find the help and advice you need quickly. We have included some specific sections in each chapter to help you find what you need.

Objectives

These should help you quickly see what each chapter will help you do. If you have a specific question or issue in mind, look through the chapter objectives to find the best match.

QTS standards

The relevant standards for Qualified Teacher Status are listed with each chapter. You can use these to plan and monitor your professional development. They may also be helpful in contributing to any self-assessment of the standards you carry out as part of your course.

Practical tasks

These are things that you can try in your teaching placement. Each teaching placement is different so not all tasks may be relevant to your situation but we hope that you will find some useful suggestions. These tasks should be small and manageable, and each should be carefully planned and reviewed. It would be a useful exercise to find three or four tasks from the book and plan when you might undertake them on teaching practice. It would also be useful to discuss these with your tutors and teachers in placement schools.

Reflective tasks

Reflection on the process of teaching and learning is a very important part of your professional development as a teacher. We have included these reflective tasks to help you focus on virtual learning as part of your wider reflections on teaching and learning. You might find it helpful to make some notes on paper while you are considering the reflective tasks.

Typical uses

These are quick notes to give you some examples of uses you can put the skills and activities to. We have made them phase specific but this is only guidance. We hope that these give you some ideas to develop into classroom projects.

Case studies

Case studies are more detailed descriptions of existing classroom practice. They help to set the context for the issues dealt with in each chapter. Some case studies come from our own experiences and some from other studies into virtual learning in classrooms.

Research summary

There is an increasing body of research into the use of virtual learning in schools and in each chapter we have selected a few examples of good quality articles, studies and reviews that should help you if you want to find out more about the topics in each chapter. In addition these would be good starting points if you were working on an assignment about virtual learning.

Chapter summary

The summaries at the end of each chapter aim to bring together the main points. You can use these to check that you have learnt what you expected from the chapter.

What next?

These are quick tips to point you in the right direction if you want to pursue the ideas in the chapter.

Useful websites

These are links to useful resources and information available on the internet.

Further reading

This is a selected reading list to support you in further research. Many of the articles and reports we have suggested are available on the web.

Glossary

There are a number of educational and technological terms use in this book – many of them are explained in the glossary at the end of the book.

Making virtual learning work for you

At the time of writing the use of VLEs in schools is just beginning. We have written this book because we are enthusiastic about the possibilities which this offers to teachers to teach in different ways. We think that virtual learning can enhance your pupils' learning experience. Making it work for you will be challenging. There is a range of technical and pedagogical barriers to success in virtual learning. However, we hope that the advice and guidance in this book will help you overcome them.

Finally, we believe that good teaching and learning have the same requirements whether it is in a traditional face-to-face classroom or in a virtual learning environment. We hope that you will find ways to make both work together through using this book.

REFERENCES REFERENCES **REFERENCES** REFERENCES **REFERENCES** REFERENCES

Becta (2003) *What the research says about virtual learning environments*. Coventry: Becta.

2
Teaching and learning using a VLE – blending face-to-face and online learning

By the end of this chapter you should be able to:

- understand the concept and core principles of blending face-to-face and online learning;
- identify what methods of learning delivery suit your pupils best;
- analyse current courses and classroom sessions and determine how using more online blended approaches can better meet the needs of you and your pupils;
- design, develop and implement online starters and plenaries;
- construct and use online peer-to-peer assessment techniques;
- develop and implement ways of using online learning in the classroom and also in the homes of your pupils;
- develop ways of getting parents involved with the online teaching and learning of their children.

This chapter addresses the following Professional Standards for QTS:

Q4, Q7, Q9, Q10, Q12, Q19, Q21, Q23, Q25

Introduction

Blended learning is not a new concept, and there are many definitions of blended learning to be found on the internet and elsewhere. What is new are the technological innovations that currently and constantly bombard education in schools, and offer increasingly innovative and ever greater opportunities for blending the teaching and learning in schools. In a blended learning environment, your pupils have access to ICT-based and online learning, and are able to draw on web-based materials in a flexible, if structured, way, to complement the more traditional face-to-face activities. It is this structuring of blended learning that is described here. (See also Chapter 3 on learning objects and Chapter 4 on using a VLE, for additional information and examples of blending online learning in schools.)

The section on useful websites at the end of this chapter has examples of the different definitions of blended learning that are out there. The Epic website (**www.epic.co.uk**) also has some extremely useful White Papers on blended learning that can be downloaded free, and which give lots of very useful background information on the subject.

Blended learning can mean a number of different things to different people. In this chapter, however, blended – sometimes called integrated – learning is defined as a mixture or combination of face-to-face and online teaching and learning activities, resources and methods to create a particular blend of learning for your pupils.

Blended learning is closely linked to the national strategy for education in schools, in which the intention is to provide a range of off- and online support for teachers and for their continuing professional development (DfES, 2005). This approach to learning enables the learner to make informed choices about which materials to use and when to use them, that is, to construct a blend that is best for them. The intention of this chapter, then, is to mirror this type of blended learning for use with your pupils in schools.

The chapter explores the ways and means by which blended learning can be implemented in schools, using the current, 'traditional', three-part lesson plan structure of starter, main activities and plenary to illustrate the different ways in which this can be done. Online peer-to-peer assessment in and out of the classroom is also discussed as a way to blend learning. There are examples of how you can get parents involved by giving ideas for online learning at home.

Each section contains explanations and examples of how to implement blended learning solutions in your own teaching practice, with real-life examples and ideas, including examples of case studies, illustrating how this is already being done in schools, and which are intended to help you achieve this with your own pupils.

REFLECTIVE TASK

How would you define blended learning for the teaching you are doing or have done on teaching practice?

Would blended learning fit in better with the ethos or available resources of any of the schools where you have done your teaching practice?

Online starter activities

The use of an online starter activity is a fairly straightforward introduction to starting to blend learning in your teaching practice. Starter activities tend to be short, usually fewer than 10 minutes, and the more interesting they are, the more interested the students are likely to be in the rest of your lesson. You could use an online activity to get the lesson off to a good start, and also to set an appropriate pace for the lesson that is tailored for the pupils in your class.

Online starter activities can also be easily differentiated to cater for the individual needs of all learners in your group, because of the flexibility of the online medium and the array of resources available to you. Examples of activities that can be conducted online are as follows.

The following idea for a starter activity for any subject at any level is one that can be differentiated for different levels of pupils, and also adapted to suit the different key stages, and the different subjects within them. It is also one which could easily be further developed to create a much longer, more involved piece of work or activity. You can ask your pupils to compare the efficacy of the different search engines available to you in your school, for example, Google or MSN.com, and compare the searching abilities of these two engines.

The idea is to pick a topic or specific words, for example, the causes of the Second World War, or the life cycle of plants, or reviews of a particular poem or book on their reading list – something that they are currently studying in class – and get them to use different search engines to find out what they can. You could split them into groups, one search engine per group, and ask them to feed back after five to ten minutes on what they have found, number of sites, information on those sites and so on. This could also be done as individuals, and as such can be differentiated for learning ability. More able pupils could be given more complex topics to search for, or be given more than one engine to use, and the reverse for lower-ability pupils, thus ensuring that all are able to complete the task at least to a certain extent. The specific details of the activity need to be tailored to meet the needs of your pupils, and to fit in to the time you have allotted for the activity at the start of the lesson. As with any new activity or resource, it is advisable to test this out yourself before asking your pupils to do it in class.

While this type of task does lend itself to a starter activity, it can also be extended and developed into a more substantial research task for project work, and this will be discussed in later sections of this chapter.

Another idea for comparison of search engines would be to use specific children's search engines.

- **Ask Jeeves For Kids at *www.askforkids.com/* is a unique service where you enter a question, and Ask Jeeves tries to point you to the right web page that provides an answer. On this site, answers have been vetted for appropriateness, and no site that is on the CyberPatrol block list is supposed to be listed. Also, if Ask Jeeves cannot answer a question, it pulls results from various search engines in its metacrawler mode.**
- **There is also KidsClick! at *www.kidsclick.org/* which is backed by librarians, and which lists about 5,000 websites in various categories.**
- **Try also Looksmart's Kids Directory at *http://search.netnanny.com/?pi=nnh3&ch=kids*. This is a listing of over 20,000 pupil-friendly websites that have been hand-picked by employees of Looksmart subsidiary Net Nanny and vetted for quality. This site also offers a safe search of the entire web, using Net Nanny software to filter Wisenut search results, as well as a free toolbar that uses the same service.**
- **There is also a version of the Yahoo search engine for children, Yahooligans, at *www.yahooligans.com/*. This is designed for children aged 7 to 12. Sites are hand-picked to be appropriate for children. Also, unlike normal Yahoo, searches will not bring back matches found by crawling the web, if there is no match from within the Yahooligan listings. This prevents possibly objectionable sites from slipping onto the screen. Also, adult-oriented banner advertising will not appear within the service.**

Other examples of online starter activities include the following.

- **Recap on previous learning by listing words relating to the topic covered in the last class on the board, and then get the pupils to use combinations of two words from the list, in Google or the preferred search engine, to see who can get the fewest websites returned from the search. This can be adapted to allow the more able pupils to move on from this and to enter their own combination of (permissible) words to see who can get the fewest websites returned; for example, try, 'conkers + slide rule'.**
- **You could put a specific website address on the board for pupils to see when they enter the classroom, and ask them to search that website for certain pieces of information – maybe a list of**

words, or a specific topic within the site – and discuss this with the whole group at the end of the activity.

- Try also *www.puzzlemaker.com* to create word searches and cryptograms for starter activities for a variety of subjects and key stages (see Chapter 4 for more of this type of site).
- Use the VLE to create and conduct a quiz for use as a starter in class. This is easily adapted for all key stages, as you could choose a variety of topics for different ages, depending on the subject you are teaching and the age group you are teaching it to. See Chapter 6 for more detailed information on the use of online assessment techniques.

CASE STUDY CASE STUDY CASE STUDY CASE STUDY CASE STUDY CASE STUDY

In a large inner-city school which currently runs the new ICT Diploma in Digital Applications (DiDA) qualification at Key Stage 4, the following is used as a starter activity in class. All pupils are given a specific website address (URL) and asked to find specific pieces of information on that website that will help them with their individual project work (for example, the Edexcel website for the DiDA from *www.edexcel.co.uk*). Differentiation is achieved by asking pupils to find more or less pieces of information in their search of the site, depending on their ability and the requirements for their coursework. Pupils are also required to feed back to the class to share their findings as well as including the results in their work.

PRACTICAL TASK PRACTICAL TASK PRACTICAL TASK PRACTICAL TASK PRACTICAL TASK

Review the face-to-face classroom starter activities that you use on your teaching practice, and decide which, if any, could be done online.

Design and try out an online starter activity.

Can it be used in your other classes, and if so, how?

REFLECTIVE TASK

Think about why you want to convert a specific part of a lesson from a face-to-face activity to an online one.

Will converting this task or activity to an online one actually enhance the learning for the students?

Online learning in the main part of the lesson

Having described a number of ways in which the start of the lesson can be transferred to an online setting, we move now to the 'middle' section of the lesson. It is not necessary to convert the whole lesson to online tasks and activities, and it is important to remember that a balance is required for all lessons (see the section on 'Getting the balance right' later in this chapter). What is given in this section are examples of ways in which parts of the main body of the lesson can be transferred to online activity.

Many subjects have project work that can easily lend itself to online learning; for example, where the internet is used as a resource for research activities. Pupils could be asked to work in groups, or pairs, to produce virtual archives for the subject they are researching, and then to present their findings to the whole class. The internet need only be one of a variety of sources for the information that they assemble and collate in a virtual archive. The power of the internet here is that it gives pupils access to a wider range of sources than has previously been possible. Not only does it provide pages of information on topics, but it may also open doors by providing avenues to other sources of information that students may not have considered before.

For example, pupils could create a virtual archive of documents and artefacts relating to a scientific discovery, such as penicillin, or the periodic table. Using the internet to search for information relating to such topics opens up scientific and historical, possibly even biographical, avenues through which to explore and add context to these discoveries. Any subject is less boring if peppered with anecdotal type evidence, and with stories of the human interactions involved with them. Adding context in this way also adds variety and interest to the facts that are being taught. Think of how much more interesting the First World War could be if you can find propaganda posters, rations lists, tales from actual battles, and so on, things that can put the facts into a more real-life context.

For revision lessons towards the end of the academic year (which also usually coincides with the end of your second teaching practice) there are a number of online alternatives to face-to-face teaching and learning strategies. The BBC website produces a vast array of revision aids (see **www.bbc.co.uk/schools/revision**) on its schools section of the site. Here you can get revision aids for all key stages, and all subjects, with sections for parents and pupils, and also games and quizzes to aid revision.

Another way to blend learning in your practice is to take your pupils to a gallery or museum which uses interactive ICT resources for displays and exhibitions. The website **www.mda.org.uk/vlmp/**, for example, has a huge list of museums with details of what you can expect when visiting them, and it might be worth considering this as part of your practice. The Eureka museum in Halifax, West Yorkshire, for example, is one such place. It offers curriculum-focused galleries (linking with the National Curriculum, QCA guidelines and science, technology, engineering and mathematics (STEM) subjects for ages 0–11) that can be used to extend and complement a number of curriculum themes.

Other museums offer virtual reality experiences; for example, the Leighton Linslade Virtual Museum at **www.leighton-museum.org.uk/** offers a virtual museum tour of its galleries with facilities for adding to the visitors' book when you've finished your virtual tour.

PRACTICAL TASK PRACTICAL TASK PRACTICAL TASK PRACTICAL TASK PRACTICAL TASK

How can you give pupils access to an appropriate knowledge base, giving them some choice in how and when to learn?

How will you receive feedback on their progress?

How you will present new knowledge in a blended learning environment?

What will be the key components of the lessons you teach?

Online peer-to-peer assessment

In this section, a number of ideas for the use of blended learning as part of a strategy to encourage peer-to-peer assessment in pupils are explored. These ideas are intended to provide a starting point only from which to create your own learning objects and activities in order to conduct peer-to-peer assessment with your own classes.

Discussion forums can be used for collaborative learning (see Chapter 4 for further details on how this can be done) and this idea can be built upon to blend peer-to-peer assessment into the classroom experience. The forums, or discussion boards (accessed via the school VLE), can act as a repository for work that you want pupils to assess and comment on, and this can be their work, or examples of more formal, referenced content, relevant to their particular course. In order to enable students to become more relaxed about this type of assessment, you might, for example, start with their assessment of formal curriculum-based information, such as exam work.

For example, you could put three exam questions onto the discussion board or forum in three separate threads. (An alternative way would be to create three separate discussion boards for the questions – it's up to you which you think might be best for your pupils.) Having set up an area – the threads – where pupils can access the questions, get them to answer each question, using messages posted for each of the threads, and make sure they pay particular attention to the marks available, and take care to answer the questions using the best strategy for the question. Strategies for answering the questions could be conducted using the interactive electronic whiteboard (IWB) as a whole-class discussion before they start the online activity.

After they have answered the questions online, get them to mark the answers posted by two other students in the class, commenting on: how they picked up the marks; where extra marks could have been picked up; and how well their strategy for answering the question actually suited the question. For example, you could get them to comment on whether or not their peers used 'over-wordy' language, and if they can match the number of points raised to the marks available, and so on.

Following on from this exercise, you could then give the pupils an area of the curriculum to study, and from which they have to set their own questions and upload them as different threads to the discussion boards. Working in groups, for example, the pupils could set questions and make up the answers, for their allotted curriculum area, deciding how many marks should be given for each one. The questions could be uploaded to the discussion boards, as different threads, and students asked to complete two other sets of questions, which have been set as different threads, as before, and receive feedback from the person who set the question, in the same way that they did for the exam questions.

From this, each pupil could then create a learning/revision resource based on their preferred learning style, and based on the feedback gained from the peer-to-peer assessment. If each group or pupil covers a different area of the curriculum, when all the work has been completed, it could be assembled in a specific area on the VLE. The end result is a resource that covers the curriculum for a whole unit, for example, that can be used by all pupils to aid learning. This is not an activity for a single lesson – as is obvious from the amount of work that can be involved – nor does it have to take up all or most of every lesson. It could be developed to span a half or full term's work on a particular unit or part unit of a course, giving pupils a more longitudinal task that relates to the teaching and learning over an extended period of time. How you chose to use an activity such as this depends on the individual requirements of your pupils.

The feedback given and received as part of the process of creating this online resource, through the peer-to-peer assessment, can be done as part of the face-to-face teaching and learning and thus blended with the ongoing online work. The IWB is one way in which you can blend the online and face-to-face peer-to-peer assessment, and which also still requires students to use the technology available to them. Pupils can provide feedback on the IWB which can then be stored electronically and uploaded to the discussion boards for later use. For homework, for example, you could ask the students to look at the feedback uploaded from the IWB and comment on it by posting feedback on the discussion boards, or by presenting their thoughts to the class the next time they meet.

CASE STUDY CASE STUDY **CASE STUDY** CASE STUDY **CASE STUDY** CASE STUDY

A large comprehensive school in the east of England has recently set up a VLE to replace their old intranet in order to enhance the ICT facilities available to staff and pupils alike from home. In addition to having access to the resources that were available on the old intranet, the system is interactive and allows a live and real-time communication between staff and pupils about their course work, revision, homework and general studies. Different departments are able to personalise the system to suit their individual departmental needs, and the control of updating and uploading course information and materials lies with each department. This is intended to speed up the process of getting the resources on to the system, and allows each department a greater range of which resources they are able to use with their pupils.

Getting parents involved – blending at home as well as in the classroom

In addition to blending learning in your classroom, you should also consider ways in which you can set online work that is to be done at home. Online 'homework' could be structured so that it involves only the individual pupil, or possibly pupils working in groups (see Chapter 4), or could involve pupils and their parents. The initial step when considering how to create a blend that involves online homework is to determine whether or not this is feasible for your pupils. You can only set this type of work if all pupils have access to a computer at home. If this is the case, there are a number of ways in which you might extend work done in the classroom to beyond the school boundaries.

Internet searches can be done as a joint effort between pupil and parent, and you may even wish to give pupils and parents differentiated words or topics to search for together. Some examples of internet-resourced learning across a number of subjects are as follows:

- Internet resources used to support project work on the First World War in Year 9 history lessons, bringing to life the facts through war posters and paintings.
- Work on geography topics such as specific countries, for example, Brazil and Italy, again in Year 9, and also rivers and flooding, in Year 8, with access to fabulous pictures of the topography and culture of the country being studied.
- In classics, internet resources can be used to support individual research on Roman life topics with Year 10 pupils, with illustrations of Roman artefacts being offered for sale at an online auction.
- In science, internet resources support the work on the solar system with Year 9 classes, and also work on ecosystems in Year 12.

PRACTICAL TASK PRACTICAL TASK PRACTICAL TASK PRACTICAL TASK PRACTICAL TASK

Set up searches for one of your placement classes – set up searches for the same topics at different levels for the different year groups and evaluate their effectiveness.

Review some source materials for your subject having done some research yourself into the information available to you – is it better than you could have produced yourself?

REFLECTIVE TASK

What do you think are the main issues for your classes and pupils when conducting internet searches?

How can you structure and focus internet-based resource activities to ensure that your pupils get the most from them in the least time?

Another idea is to set up a live 'chat' session for pupils and parents to join in from home. This could be used to discuss the course or topic itself, or to get parents involved in the subject more by giving their experiences of working in that area, for example. You might be able to get pupils whose parents work in specific industries, such as science or business and so on, to join a chat session and talk about their experiences in the 'real' world.

In a similar way, you could set up discussion boards for pupils and parents and ask that each pupil and parent add messages to the board to stimulate or continue discussions started in class.

Also, if the school has an intranet that can be accessed from home, you might consider setting up an area so that parents are able to monitor the progression of their child or children in the subjects they are taking with you through access to the school site.

PRACTICAL TASK PRACTICAL TASK PRACTICAL TASK PRACTICAL TASK PRACTICAL TASK

Find out about the intranet or VLE facilities available to you in the school.

Can you use them to set up online tasks for homework as described above?

If so, how will you do this and what will you set up with the different classes that you teach?

Online plenaries

There are a number of different ways in which the face-to-face plenary activities or tasks can be converted into online ones. Like starters, plenaries are fairly short activities or tasks, usually fewer than 10 minutes in duration, and like starter activities they are a good starting point for your introduction to blending face-to-face with online learning.

Plenary activities usually involve a review of learning with the whole group, and can often take the form of a question-and-answer (Q/A) session, with you directing questions as necessary, depending on the relative progress of specific students. The online medium is a useful tool for reviewing or recapping the learning done within a particular lesson, to check what you (and they) have covered in class. It can also be used as an interesting and interactive tool to check if your pupils have understood what has been taught.

Quizzes are one way to convert a face-to-face Q/A session into the online medium. This can take the form of a quiz done on the whiteboard with the whole class, or you could get pupils to log on to a specific quiz site and complete the questions as individuals. If the school has its own VLE, you could construct your own quiz for particular lessons and use it for formative assessment as you work through the syllabus with your pupils.

The internet has a wealth of information on online quizzes that can be used for teaching in schools. These include the following.

- *www.schoolhistory.co.uk/teachers/plenaries.html* has information and ideas for all key stages and also a specific section for teachers with ideas for starters and plenaries in history.
- *www.channel4.com/learning/teachers/websites/* has a variety of websites for use by teachers and pupils, and includes interactive activities aimed at stimulating and engaging students of a wide range of abilities and levels.
- *www.quia.com* has a collection of shared online activities and quizzes in more than 150 categories, and provides a variety of services for educators which include tools for creating different types of online activities.
- One other major resource for plenary activities is the BBC website (at *www.bbc.co.uk/schools/*) which has a 'bitesize' section for providing revision aids for the subjects in the different key stages. It also has a particularly colourful interactive games section for schools, *www.bbc.co.uk/schools/games*, which allows you to pick a combination of subject and age range and then take a quiz in a topic of your choice.

The above list is not exhaustive; rather, it should be used as a starting point for research into the type of tools that best suit the way you want to teach and which you can adapt for your pupils.

If your school has a VLE and if it is using web logs, or blogs, with pupils, then another example for a plenary activity would be to give pupils five to ten minutes at the end of a lesson to record their thoughts and progress for the topic you have just taught in their own personalised blog. This may be more useful for the later key stages, and is also a useful way to get pupils to become more independent reflective learners. Chapter 7 has details on blogs for schools.

CASE STUDY CASE STUDY CASE STUDY CASE STUDY CASE STUDY CASE STUDY

A large inner-city comprehensive school in the north of England uses web logs with Year 12 and 13 students at Key Stage 5. The students are required to produce their project work as a website, and to record their progress in the form of a blog, and they are given time to do this in school. They are also able to update their blog from home through the school's VLE system.

PRACTICAL TASK PRACTICAL TASK PRACTICAL TASK PRACTICAL TASK PRACTICAL TASK

Review the face-to-face classroom plenaries that you use on your teaching practice, and decide which, if any, could be done online.

Design and try out an online plenary.

Review and evaluate the websites available for creating online quizzes and also those that provide ready-made ones.

Which ones are most applicable to your teaching practice?

REFLECTIVE TASK

REFLECTIVE TASK

Did your online plenary work better than a similar activity that was done face to face?

If so, why, and if not, why not – how could you have done it better?

Getting the balance right

Most adults find it difficult to sit at a computer and work alone for extended periods of time without a break. This is something that is even harder for pupils to do, and something which needs to be taken into account when blending the face-to-face learning with individual online learning tasks. Online activities should be broken up with other methods of teaching and learning. Any good teacher deploys a range of resources, techniques and methods in any one lesson in order to stimulate learning, and this is no different for blending online with face-to-face teaching and learning. Getting the balance right is something that takes practice, and may be very different for the different groups that you teach. Chapter 7 has further details on this aspect of blended learning.

PRACTICAL TASK PRACTICAL TASK PRACTICAL TASK PRACTICAL TASK PRACTICAL TASK

When thinking about how to blend face-to-face with online teaching and learning, that is, when considering how to construct a blend for your pupils, you need to try to answer the following questions:

- Who are the learners (key stage, level, age) and will they need to change their attitudes in order to embrace online learning?
- What is the culture of the school and will this need to change and adapt?
- What new strategies, pedagogical issues, procedures or techniques do you need to learn to do this?
- How much time do you have for planning and preparing this and do the learners have enough time to complete the tasks you have set?
- How well do your blends, your online tasks, fit in with the scheme of work and lesson plans for the syllabus your students are following?
- Do you have the resources available to you and to them for what you are trying to achieve?

Issues with online learning

We all know children who can spend hours playing computer games, but how many of us know children who can concentrate for so long at school? The quality of the online materials that you use in class is important, and you need to ensure that it is interesting and exciting enough to hold the attention of the pupils for whatever tasks you have set them to do. Make sure you review any online materials before you use them in class, as pupils have a low tolerance of materials that fall short of the ones they can get on their video games. With this kind of medium, learners will expect to be entertained while learning and are unlikely to respond to anything less. Research into this area has revealed a number of aspects of learning through gaming technology that you may be able to exploit (see **www.futurela-b.org.uk**). Strategies for use of the internet as a resource like this need to be very specific and focused in order to avoid the problem of pupils getting lost trying to find the information they need, or getting distracted by banners offering other services. Pupils may require more intervention from you to enable them to discern and extract relevant information from online sources than would have been the case in face-to-face textbook-type lessons (Deaney et al, 2006).

You also need to be sure that when they do use search engines to find websites containing useful information, that information is pitched at the right level and is accessible to them. It can take as long to look through a search engine list as it does to look up index entries in a book. To be successful, information-seeking activities within the classroom need to be very clearly structured and focused.

Parental involvement

One issue with parental involvement in online learning is that of the hardware and software differences in the homes of your pupils. For pupils who live in homes without broadband connections, there may be an issue of access with this kind of homework if they are using the telephone line for long periods of time. Another issue with parental involvement is that of the computer skills of the parents, resulting in even the most minor of technical faults possibly being barriers to the access to the computer for the pupils. Issues of access need to be monitored in this way so as not to cause problems for the pupils when setting this type of work (Boulton, 2006).

There are additional management issues that also need to be considered when planning to use online technology in your lessons. You will need to think about:

- **which classrooms you can use with the appropriate technology already there;**
- **whether or not you can use the ICT rooms on a regular basis for your teaching;**
- **how to plan teaching for the different layouts that often accompany these rooms;**
- **what changes you may need to make to your own teaching style and the pedagogical methods you usually deploy when teaching using mainly ICT;**
- **whether there are adequate technical backup and resources for the activities you have planned;**
- **whether or not your own understanding and skills of the resources you are going to use are adequate for what you are trying to do.**

REFLECTIVE TASK

Are you up to the tasks you have set with ICT – do you need further training?

What are the gaps in your own knowledge and how will you address them?

Think about how you will engage the pupils and ensure that the goals are clear to them.

Think about how you will evaluate the online teaching and learning strategies, activities and tasks that you use.

RESEARCH SUMMARY RESEARCH SUMMARY **RESEARCH SUMMARY** RESEARCH SUMMARY

Recent research indicates that teachers draw on the wide range of internet resources available to broaden classroom resources and references to bring the reality of the outside into the classroom (Deaney et al, 2006). This research also indicates that a concern for teachers is that of offering a balance between offering learners more security but risking similar task outcomes, and providing opportunities for greater independence but risking pupil confusion about task requirements (Deaney et al, 2006). Hence the need to balance the online and face-to-face activities, and to balance control

with structure, with allowing for flexibility and individuality in pupils. The need for differentiated tasks is also indicated as a requirement by many teachers for this kind of pupil activity (Deaney et al, 2006). Ways of differentiating the various activities and tasks have been provided throughout this chapter in order to offer ways to alleviate this potential problem.

CHAPTER **SUMMARY**

This chapter has presented a number of strategies and ideas for blending face-to-face and online learning in schools.

There are a number of practical ways in which this can be done, and examples of these have been offered as a way forward for you to try in your schools during teaching practice.

There is no right or wrong way to do this, and thus the best way forward is to start to blend your teaching activities, try them on your pupils, and evaluate them through reflective iterative practice, until you find what works for you with your pupils.

What next?

From here you could adapt your teaching methods to incorporate more online learning strategies, tasks and activities and move on to integrating these within a virtual learning environment, or the school intranet (see Chapter 4 for further details of how this can be done).

Useful websites

Some definitions of blended learning can be found at the following websites.

- An increasingly popular combination of online and in-person, classroom learning activities. *www.cybermediacreations.com/elearning/glossary.htm*
- An educational formation that integrates e-learning techniques including online delivery of materials through web pages, discussion boards and/or email with traditional teaching methods including lectures, in-person discussions, seminars, or tutorials. *www.teach-nology.com/glossary/terms/b/*
- Learning or training events or activities where e-learning, in its various forms, is combined with more traditional forms of training such as 'classroom' training. *www.intelera.com/glossary.htm*
- Using ICT as appropriate alongside traditional methods such as discussion or face-to-face teaching. *www.itslifejimbutnotasweknowit.org.uk/lt_glossary.htm*
- Blended learning is the combination of multiple approaches to teaching or to educational processes which involve the deployment of a diversity of methods and resources or to learning experiences which are derived from more than one kind of information source. Examples include combining technology-based materials and traditional print materials, group and individual study, structured pace study and self-paced study, tutorial and coaching. *http://en.wikipedia.org/wiki/Blended_learning*
- Website with resources and advice for teachers: *www.gamelearning.net*, also, reviews of games and learning can be found at *www.futurelab.org.uk/research/lit_reviews*

Also:
- *www.epic.co.uk* is a very useful site with lots of free downloadable reports on e-learning and blended learning – a site worth exploring for background information on this topic.
- *www.teach-nology.com/* also has a range of free and easy-to-use resources for teachers with lesson plans, worksheets, games and tips, and also a space to share your online ideas with other teachers.
- *www.terry-freedman.org.uk* is a site set up with lots of practical advice and articles for educationalists.
- *http://stiveshaslemere.com/mgb/Coming_of_age.pdf* is a very comprehensive online book – *Coming of age: an introduction to the new world wide web* – of case studies and how-to articles edited by Terry Freedman, and contributed to by leading practitioners in the world of education. The book also has a very useful glossary.
- *http://elgg.net* is an open-source personal learning landscape for users and developers of e-learning. The emphasis of the site is focused very much on the learner, and on communities of learners, aiming to give them the means to control and own their own development and growth through the use of everyday web technologies.

REFERENCES REFERENCES REFERENCES REFERENCES **REFERENCES** REFERENCES

Boulton, H (2006) *Managing e-learning: What are the real implications for schools?* Nottingham Trent University.

Deaney, R, Ruthven, K and Hennessey, S (2006) Teachers developing 'practical theories' of the contribution of information and communication technologies to subject teaching and learning: an analysis of cases from English secondary schools, *British Educational Research Journal*, 32, 459–480.

DfES (2005) *Harnessing technology: transforming learning and children's services*. London: Department for Education and Skills.

FURTHER READING FURTHER READING **FURTHER** READING FURTHER READING

Bloxham, S, Twiselton, S and Jackson, A (2005) *Challenges and opportunities: Developing learning and teaching in ITE across the UK*. ESCalate ITE Project. St Martin's College, Lancaster, ESCalate.

Facer, K (2005) Could computer games help to transform the way we learn?, *Vision* (Issue 1). Futurelab, at www.futurelab.org.uk

3
Learning objects

By the end of this chapter you should be able to:

- understand the range of learning objects available;
- explore the options and variants of a variety of learning objects;
- suggest typical uses for a wide variety of learning objects across phases;
- state some advantages and disadvantages of each learning object discussed;
- select appropriate learning objects for inclusion in your school setting;
- create a collection of learning objects which addresses different teaching and learning styles in different phases and schools, and includes opportunity for assessment of learning and assessment for learning;
- demonstrate awareness of the advantages and disadvantages of learning objects when planning the use of a VLE within your own school setting.

This chapter addresses the following Professional Standards for QTS:
Q4 , Q6, Q8, Q10, Q12, Q14, Q16, Q22, Q24, Q25, Q30

Introduction to learning objects

Pupil interaction with a VLE, at whatever age, is through a variety of learning objects. These can be customised to suit the needs of the pupil and the teacher and vary from course to course according to the teacher's preference. The way you choose to use the learning objects will reflect the teaching and learning styles of yourself and your groups, as well as their personalised learning agenda. By utilising the range of learning objects described in this chapter as a part of your everyday teaching, and giving access to parents/carers and other interested bodies, you are also working towards addressing aspects of the *Every Child Matters* (DfES, 2004) agenda.

Assignments

For many courses, assignments are an integral part. They often form part of the final course work for a wide range of vocational and academic courses. By using the various facilities available via the VLE it is possible to provide excellent support for your students. Detailed examples of how these can be used are given below.

Deadlines

When you are setting a piece of work, or an assignment using your VLE, you should include a deadline. This is good experience for primary pupils as it enables them to become used to the deadline systems related to secondary school education. At secondary school level it helps to develop autonomy and independent learning. With most VLE systems it is possible to include start dates and end dates for assignments. Once these have been entered, they are automatically linked to the calendar. It is good practice to encourage your pupils to explore the calendar. You might want to consider starter activities for your lessons that will encourage your pupils to do this.

It is important to remember that where the submission is linked to final exam board course work, further submission may not be allowed. If this is the case you can set the VLE to stop further submissions. Schools will usually have a policy of how many times a piece of exam board course work can be submitted – with some VLEs it is possible to set this up. However, the majority of assessment is likely to be formative, requiring that the pupil will be able to enter into a cycle of submission, feedback, target setting and modification.

Online assignments

This facility requires the pupil to provide a response to a stimulus, for example an exam question or course work requirement. Once you have created the support materials and the assignment, the pupils can work through the task(s) using the VLE and linked resources. Once they have completed their work, or at the end of a session/module, they can then upload their work for you to provide feedback. Ideally you will ensure the uploading is carried out frequently. Research has shown that students who receive regular feedback on their progress will achieve more, i.e. formative feedback, or assessment for learning. (Black and Wiliam, 1998)

The VLE allows you to add comments to their work and set targets for improvement. Most VLEs also have a facility where the pupils can set their own targets, based on your feedback and the criteria they are working to. This in turn opens up a firm basis for dialogue, perso- nalised learning and an opportunity for pupils to improve their performance iteratively.

Typical uses
Primary: Pupils submitting small tasks for a range of subject areas. While these are going to be smaller than at secondary level, they provide an opportunity for primary pupils to develop the skills necessary at secondary level. This facility can prove very useful when Year 6 pupils are working through bridging units in preparation for their secondary school transfer.
Secondary: Pupils submitting course work or tasks towards course work.

Text assignments

These are very useful for short pieces of work. The pupil completes the piece of work via the VLE without the need to use other software, i.e. in text. In primary schools it might be an image that is used, and the pupils are prompted to do some investigative work, e.g. a linked science project, or 'tell a story' as part of the literacy hour. At secondary level it might be a critical piece of text about a poem that is being studied in English, an evaluation of a completed piece of work, or planning a D&T project. The pupil then uploads the text for the teacher to view, who in turn responds with feedback. This can be in either plain text or rich text, depending on your requirements and the formatting facilities available.

As an addition, this facility can be used for individual target setting and development of work in progress.

For differentiation, when using this with less able pupils, those with special needs or English as an additional language (EAL), it may be necessary to provide a writing framework to provide scaffolding for them to complete the task(s).

Offline assignments

This is where the pupil hands in a piece of work as hard copy, i.e. not via the VLE. The teacher then provides feedback via the VLE. This is excellent for pupils who present their work visually or create a product that cannot be submitted in any other form than as an artefact. This could take the form of a project in resistant materials, art, graphics, etc. At the primary level this could be used for a whole variety of project work within Key Stage 1 and Key Stage 2 curricula. As you then mark this work and provide the written feedback, you can share future targets with individual pupils, and record your feedback in the VLE. This helps to develop a record that you can both access.

The flexible nature of assessment means that almost anything can be assessed, targets set and recorded, and feedback provided. One of the great advantages for the teacher is that there is an ongoing record of progress, and for pupils, they can access their targets at any time, which is particularly useful when they start their next project. However, no evidence of the actual assessed work exists on the VLE and as the feedback system is usually based on plain text, it is not possible to record the product as an electronic image.

Typical uses

Primary: Offline assignments can be used in a similar way as at secondary level, but setting up an emailing alert system can be more problematic because of the access to email by younger pupils. Teachers will need to be aware of issues of pupil's skills.

Secondary: The pupil produces work, which the teacher then marks and provides feedback and individual targets, via the VLE. A system of emailing the pupil to let them know when the teacher feedback is available can also be set up automatically via most VLEs.

Workshop

This is a specialised form of assignment where pupils submit their work and are then presented with a combination of their own and other pupils' work to assess, or just other pupils' work, or just their own – depending on your learning objectives and how you are managing peer observation and individual target setting. Options can be set to limit the number of assessments each pupil has to make, whether the teacher has to 'pass' the first assessment the pupil makes, and whether the pupil has to assess their own work. This facility fits very neatly into national strategies whereby peer evaluation is encouraged, as is review of individual targets. It also fits into personalised learning, in terms of setting own targets, and the principles of *Every Child Matters* where target setting is of great importance.

Typical uses

Primary: Teachers and pupils can use this tool to comment on how other pupils have described characters in a shared story or reviewing each other's work and comment on techniques used in art.

Secondary: This tool can be used for following an assignment where pupils have produced a summary, for example of a chapter of a book. In addition pupils can submit their work and are

---

asked to assess their own and three other pieces of work using criteria supplied at the start of the assignment.

Gradebook

This item records the marks and grades given from assignments, quizzes and other learning objects. The grades can usually be viewed within the VLE or exported to other programs such as spreadsheets for further analysis. The grades can be used to provide evidence of attainment and progression.

REFLECTIVE TASK

Think about a group you have taught recently where you have recorded marks. How these could be used with your group to set individual targets for development? Would you need to make any changes to the structure of your record sheet? If you have access to a VLE and have some recorded marks, add these to an offline task, and then using these for target setting.

Typical uses
Gradebooks are an excellent tool to use with pupils in both primary and secondary phases when reviewing progress or target setting. It is also useful to have this information in one place when reporting to parents. The grades are essential for informing both short- and long-term planning.

Choice

Most VLE systems allow some form of voting and displaying of results. This can be an excellent resource for lessons on citizenship and PSHE. Once the voting has taken place, graphs and responses are produced automatically, with options to allow pupils to see only their own responses, or the overall responses of the class, year group, school, etc. Some schools have used this to make decisions about lunch facilities, décor for new pupil areas, policy decisions, etc. It can be very wide ranging and used at all levels in the school. It is definitely worth experimenting with. If you are responsible for a form group or for PSHE you might want to set up a link to a discussion area, from a choice object, whereby the pupils can discuss a specific issue, then vote on it, or vice versa. This can be very motivating for the pupils and reflects the growth in interactive television programmes that pupils, even those who are disaffected with school, can relate to.

Typical uses
In primary and secondary phases this can be used when voting for representatives of a school council. It provides rapid acquisition of data in an easily understood display. It reflects inter-active television, which is within the experience of the vast majority of pupils. It can be very motivating and exciting as pupils watch the results coming in, again reflecting developments on television. This can be a good way for pupils to explore their fears and insecurities about certain topics while remaining anonymous. On the other hand, this object could become 'boring' if overused in the classroom, for example having a vote at the end of every PSHE lesson.

Calendar facility

Encouraging pupils to meet deadlines can be time-consuming and difficult. There will be many different learning styles in each group you teach: some of your pupils will plan their time carefully to ensure they are not working right up to the final deadline; others will not start their work until it is almost the final deadline. However, pupils are increasingly motivated by accessing their assignment work through the internet via a VLE. The calendar facility can be used to support all of your pupils, breaking down the final piece of course work into manageable sections with deadlines, and reminding pupils of what they should be completing by when.

Most VLE systems enable pupils to access more information by clicking on the date, which then links to details of the assignment. In turn this links to URLs for additional information, support materials for the less able or EAL pupils, and guidance on how to meet the awarding body's criteria. With challenging groups, the idea of accessing assignment requirements via a VLE can be more stimulating and can help with classroom management.

Typical uses

Primary: This facility can be used for informing pupils and parents of forthcoming school events and due dates for class projects and other events.

Secondary: It might also be used to share deadlines for quizzes and assignments. This can be subject or whole-school related. Parents and pupils can access the information. Most systems automatically copy deadlines into the calendar and provide personalised calendars for each pupil. But not all pupils will remember, or be motivated, to use this facility. Aim to build the use of the calendar into your lessons to help to build this into the routines of your groups.

Forum

Forums allow discussions between teachers and pupils, or between pupils. As the discussions are asynchronous, the initial post and the responses are available to be viewed for as long as required. This has great advantages for questions about academic matters which will prove to be of use to future pupils.

Some excellent uses of this are related to the transition from Key Stage 2 to Key Stage 3. Pupils have different concerns about their transition and these can be alleviated to some extent through setting up a forum between the secondary and primary schools. As the teacher, you can set up specific forums, such as discussions on first day, first term, lessons, making friends, etc. Getting Year 7 pupils to interact with Year 6 pupils can be extremely effective. You are able to monitor the forums as they develop, helping you in your involvement with, and understanding of, the transition period.

Within curriculum subjects, forums can also be used in relation to course work, exam revision or preparation for lessons in the citizenship and PSHE curriculum. With the latter, some VLEs allow you to set up forums that allow only certain pupils to access them. This then allows pupils working on specific topics or in specific groups to prepare an argument for or against an aspect, or to prepare a presentation on a related topic. The whole concept of using the asynchronous discussion facility is very motivating for pupils.

When using the forum facility with pupils it is important to set ground rules from the outset. These should reflect the school's policies. For example, you need to consider how you will manage unacceptable language or bullying. Some pupils may want to communicate using mobile phone language. Will you accept this? Does this reflect the development of their English language? Will you be able to understand it? If you are willing to accept this language, will it stop some groups from being able to access the discussion, such as EAL pupils?

PRACTICAL TASK PRACTICAL TASK PRACTICAL TASK PRACTICAL TASK PRACTICAL TASK

Devise a set of ground rules for pupils using a forum.

As with many aspects of using VLEs, it is beneficial to introduce pupils to the forum facility early on in their school life. The system is generally very simple to use and can be understood easily by pupils at Key Stage 2. To encourage pupils to make sensible contributions, you can encourage them to comment within a forum on a specific topic, for example a discussion related to a poem in literacy, or a contribution towards a history topic such as the Second World War, where pupils can rate each other's contributions. This needs to be handled sensitively, but peer evaluation is encouraged and is a skill to be developed; this is another method of developing and sharing these skills.

CASE STUDY CASE STUDY CASE STUDY CASE STUDY CASE STUDY CASE STUDY

A large comprehensive school in north Nottinghamshire worked to develop links with feeder schools to smooth the transition for their Year 6 pupils. Two teachers from the secondary school worked with the Year 6 teachers to develop a forum, linking pupils between the two schools.

Training was needed to set up and manage the forum, which was done after school. The primary teachers were unfamiliar with the VLE set-up, but after a short session on what the VLE was, how to set up the forum facility and how to give their pupils access, they were confident in the technical aspects. The software for the VLE was already being used in the secondary school, so all that the primary school required was an internet connection.

A meeting was held initially so that the teachers could identify how they wanted to use the forum facility and to look at issues such as pedagogy, pupil skills and capability needed, etc. Once they were clear on their objectives a small group of pupils was chosen to pilot the forum.

The forum allowed Year 6 pupils to ask questions of Year 7 pupils regarding their concerns about the transition between key stages, and schools. This proved valuable for both the passive and active members of the forum. It also resulted in the primary pupils being familiar with the VLE being used in their future secondary school, which again proved to be beneficial in the transfer.

Once the initial pilot had proved to be successful it was rolled out to the whole of the Year 6 and Year 7 groups. An evaluation took place and it was found to be so beneficial to the transition process that it has now been rolled out to all the feeder schools. Initially this was a concern because of the number of Year 6 pupils that could potentially be asking questions, but it has been found that their concerns tend to be similar, so questions are left up for all the pupils to share.

The school is now looking to develop its links further by working with the primary feeder schools to implement common bridging units for core subjects. These will be started in Year 6 and developed in Year 7 – again helping with the transition process.

Typical uses

Primary: This tool can be used to set up groups to prepare a presentation on a current topic. The VLE enables pupils to continue with their preparation outside lesson time, or via a 'web environment', thereby encouraging new skills and independent learning.

Secondary: Pupils can ask questions of the teacher about revision topics in which they are not confident. This can also be used for discussion between group members engaged in group work, and as a social forum with relaxed rules on discussion topics is often used as a 'hook' in order to encourage pupil use of the VLE.

Glossary

Some VLEs allow the option of adding a glossary. This involves defining certain key words and their meanings. Any mention of these words in assignments, etc., automatically generates a link to the word definition. As the teacher you need to set up the glossary, although there are some available for download for certain topics. This can be an excellent facility, particularly to encourage understanding by less able pupils, but also in building an understanding of key words and key concepts.

Typical uses

Primary: This tool can be used to list key words that are being focused on during that term or key words that link to current topics. It can also be used to support pupils' understanding of terms linked to concepts that are not easily understood.

Secondary: The glossary can be used for key words and key concepts related to different subjects; building up 'jargon' for use in examinations.

PRACTICAL TASK PRACTICAL TASK PRACTICAL TASK PRACTICAL TASK PRACTICAL TASK

Choose a topic which will be developed for use in your VLE and write a list of key words. The relevant National Strategy documents will be of use here. Once the list is complete, add the meanings of these key words in pupil language, to form the basis of a glossary.

As you progress through the topic you can continue to add to the glossary as you identify concepts that are not being understood, or that are being consistently mis-spelled. With most systems, the glossary can be retained from year to year and saved as part of the course. It can be time-consuming to set up the glossary, but this is outweighed by the benefits to pupils.

Lesson

This can replace teacher input, and is therefore appropriate for schools where distance learning is being encouraged. It is also appropriate for use with concepts pupils find difficult to understand. You may want to use this object for lesson support, or as an opportunity for pupils to revisit lesson theory either on their own, at home, or, particularly for primary pupils, with their parents/carers.

The lesson comprises a collection of pages – essentially web pages – which have an assessment component at the end. As pupils read the information and undertake the tasks, they acquire knowledge and understanding, which they apply to the assessment at the end of the page. The result of this assessment determines which page the pupil sees next.

The pupil is presented with a series of pages of information which are targeted at their level of understanding, thus taking a step towards personalised learning, while at the same time developing independent learning skills.

PRACTICAL TASK PRACTICAL TASK **PRACTICAL TASK** PRACTICAL TASK **PRACTICAL TASK**

Setting up a lesson

It is useful to plan the 'lesson' on paper before creating it on the VLE. Start by collecting the resources which will be presented to the pupils. Arrange these into an appropriate order and draw progressive links between them. As assessments will be used to gauge progression through the topic, links need to be drawn after the end of each section to where the pupil will be taken to if they need additional support.

When you set up the lesson you can ensure that the content is presented at an appropriate level for your groups of pupils. The content is far better matched to pupil ability than with a standard assignment. Autonomous learning is promoted – to the extent that true distance learning is possible. Parents can sit with and support their children in working through your lessons, particularly at the primary school level, to ensure their understanding. However, creating a lesson is a lot more time-consuming than with other forms of assignment. But don't let the idea of having to create materials with end assessment be daunting. You will already have banks of worksheets and assessment sheets that you use in class. Just think of the advantages both to yourself and your pupils, of putting these onto a web environment that can be accessed in your lessons as remedial work, or extension work, or from home to go through work in class, or used for revision purposes before end-of-key-stage tests, or exam board tests.

Typical uses

Primary: This tool can be used in moving pupils through a concept in mathematics, such as fractions, that can be difficult to understand.

Secondary: It is useful for guiding pupils through a conceptually difficult topic related to the subject, such as the Data Protection Act in ICT, or the way muscles work in PE.

Quiz

All VLEs provide some facility for online automated assessment. Most offer various question types and assessment modes. For formative assessment, quizzes can provide helpful feedback, along with the option to revisit questions to refine answers until correct. If structured well, they can be very motivating for pupils of all abilities. For summative assessment, various options can be set which allow only one attempt, for example, and can limit attempts to certain times of the day to simulate external examinations or end-of-key-stage tests. Some VLEs also have the facility to shuffle the order of questions and answers, an excellent facility if you are using it with a full class, as opportunities for cheating are reduced.

All VLEs offer a variety of different question types.

- **Multiple-choice questions.** These allow for uncomplicated assessment with single or multiple correct answers. Many systems also have a variation of this which will allow pupils to select true or false answers for a particular statement.
- **Short-answer questions.** These prompt for a single word or short sentence. There is little tolerance for mistakes, although alternative answers can often be supplied.
- **Numerical questions.** These require a single numerical answer. The main difference between this question type and the short-answer type is that a numerical question can have an inbuilt level of tolerance in the answer. For example, a correct answer may be specified as one between 5.5 and 6.7. Some systems also allow the use of random numbers, so that each student would receive a question which is unique, reducing the ability to copy answers.
- **Matching questions.** These consist of several sub-questions to which the pupil must select the correct answers to each question. These questions may also be used to match two halves of a sentence or put a series of logical steps in order.

Most systems allow some sort of facility to select questions randomly from a bank in order to build different quizzes for each pupil.

It is usually possible to build up a bank of questions and to categorise the questions so that it is possible to build a quiz from a certain category. For example, at the primary school level you could set up quizzes for each mathematical topic taught in a week/month, then very quickly select certain questions from each of these quizzes for an end-of-term test to see what knowledge has been retained by the pupils. In the same way it is simple to create questions in secondary subjects that relate to different awarding body modules, then mix and match these for an end-of-term test before reporting to parents on the term's progress.

Images can usually be incorporated within quizzes so that questions can be based upon them. This can be particularly useful if you want to ask questions about a specific diagram, such as for biology, or a painting in art, or a network configuration in ICT.

PRACTICAL TASK PRACTICAL TASK PRACTICAL TASK PRACTICAL TASK PRACTICAL TASK

Plan a quiz that you could use in your teaching. Consider the group, curriculum, and their abilities. Aim to use different types of questions such as multiple choice, matching, and short answer. If you have access to a VLE, implement the quiz and pilot it with a small group of pupils.

Typical uses
Primary: To prepare pupils for end-of-key-stage tests; for use as formative assessment or summative assessment; for use in plenary sessions.
Secondary: Pupils often view this as a fun activity as they compete with themselves or their peer group with scores and times. It can save you time in marking work – the results are available to the pupil and the teacher, which is very useful in tutorials, and for personalised target setting. As evidence of assessment of knowledge with some qualifications, e.g. BTEC. As a starter activity, particularly where it is important to establish current knowledge before moving to new knowledge.

Text page

A simple text page is a useful way of conveying small amounts of information to pupils. Some formatting options such as font type and colour, etc., may be possible with some systems. Images cannot be inserted.

Typical uses
Primary: Instructions for homework, or a piece of work that is to be completed in class. Background information for a new project, or extension work.
Secondary: Provide an extract of a mark scheme for a piece of course work; provide information on a topic that has been covered; use case studies for homework or additional work for the more able.

Web page

Although designing a web page may sound daunting, most systems use a WYSIWYG (what you see is what you get) editor to simplify design. Although a full website can be designed using this feature, most teachers find the web page resource most useful as being a simple way to produce a well formatted page of information or stimulus material. See Figure 3.1.

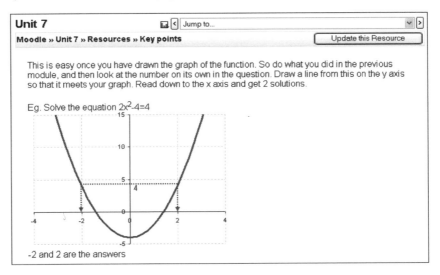

Figure 3.1

Most systems use controls that will be familiar to any word-processor user. As it is a web page, images and hyperlinks may be included. If you have advanced skills you can create the HTML in a web design package or text editor, and then copy and paste it into the VLE web page. As you can use images and a greater number of formats, fonts and colours than with the text page facility, this is more appropriate for the less able and those for whom English is a second language. For the more able, inserting hyperlinks to additional information or extension work is simple and quick to do. As the current younger generation enjoy using the computer and, particularly, 'surfing the web', this can be an excellent way of motivating pupils to work.

When designing your web page it is important to remember basic web design principles:

- **Consider the download time and don't use too many graphic images – or large graphic images.**
- **Consider the colours with respect to your audience.**
- **White backgrounds can look very professional.**
- **Consider the interests and abilities of your group when selecting colours, text and fonts.**
- **A good tip is to look at websites that your pupils enjoy, and aim to mirror their layout and design style.**
- **There are many sites on the internet that can help you with web design if you want to focus on this aspect.**

Some schools might use the internet as a reward at the end of lessons. If you are a student teacher this can be difficult, and can become an issue when you are trying to do a plenary in your lesson. Using this facility can be a compromise by setting up web pages yourself that fit into the objectives of the lesson, and link to your plenary, while providing the facility of using the web pages. Advantages include that this can provide a relatively simple way to produce a student-friendly page of content. Pupils really enjoy learning and working with the internet, so this facility can be very motivating. You also can upload resources that you have already produced in electronic format and there is an increasing range of software that can produce diagrams simply and easily, which can then be uploaded.

Typical uses

Primary: A wide range of opportunities to develop independent learning skills, while providing pupils with the opportunity to use the internet. A range of topics can be uploaded and used for supporting the less able, or providing extension work for the more able. Help sheets can also be uploaded for pupils to refer to, thereby freeing the teacher to provide support for those that require it.

Secondary: Producing a page of content about a specific topic, including images and more complex text formatting.

Link to file

One of the key features of a VLE is the ability to share a range of resources: presentations, word-processed files, images/photos, concept maps, exam questions, video, audio files, music, etc. A simple way of doing this is by using the 'link to file' facility. This works by providing some text or icon, which, when clicked on, opens a file (see Figure 3.2). The file to be linked to can either be stored within the VLE system itself, on the local network, or on the internet. Storing it on the local network will mean, however, that the file will not be available when the resource is accessed from home or any other network.

Typical uses

Primary: This can be used for providing an audio file containing a piece of poetry for the pupils to discuss in class. A video clip of a traffic light control system when introducing the topic of control in ICT would be another suitable subject.

Secondary: Examples could include: providing students with a video file, containing a summary of the current topic; sharing music which can then be commented on; or sharing a video which pupils need to watch, then prepare a report on, e.g. the Holocaust.

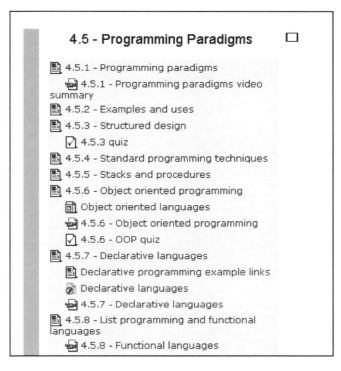

Figure 3.2

Link to website

Part of the sharing resources paradigm of VLEs is the facility to link to other web pages. This is invaluable in allowing pupils easy access to sites of value to them. You can limit the number of web pages for the less able, supporting them by providing clear guidelines on how to access them, and what type of information to look for. The more able can be provided with additional links that will enable them to access higher key stage levels, or levels in external exams.

PRACTICAL TASK PRACTICAL TASK **PRACTICAL TASK** PRACTICAL TASK **PRACTICAL TASK**

Choose a topic you have taught recently and list all of the websites that you used during the planning and delivery. Search the internet for valid and reliable consolidation resources. If you have access to a VLE, create a section and add these links into it. With most VLEs, you will be able to monitor the amount of access by your pupils.

Consider the variety of resources that can be made available to the pupils. Websites can be checked before they are used to make sure they are both appropriate and suitable for the age of the pupils. It is possible to cache your websites so that the access is speeded up in lessons. However, links must be checked regularly to ensure that the link is still working. Some VLEs notify you when the web links are broken.

> **Typical uses**
> Primary: Pupils can often spend too long searching on the internet. While it is important they develop these skills, you can speed up the process of finding relevant information by providing a range of websites for them to access. This can be used for specific curriculum-related projects such as electricity, or Egypt; or for projects that relate to school productions.
> Secondary: Giving pupils links to useful sites that they could use for a research project following a specific topic.

Dialogue

This facility enables a one-to-one asynchronous dialogue between pupil and teacher. This typically works by one party initiating the conversation, causing a popup or other notification on the other party's screen when they log on. In this way, a conversation can develop over time. This could serve as a target-setting and feedback mechanism, a way of providing help for coursework, mentoring tutor group members, etc.

Dialogue can be particularly beneficial for pupils who find it difficult to contribute in class, or who prefer to think carefully about what they are saying before they say it. Pupils may also want to discuss topics that are confidential to them but are unable to do so face to face. However, this can be very time-consuming for the teacher if a number of dialogues are ongoing concurrently. Some colleges are looking at case-loading where this is increasingly being used, i.e. time is being allocated per student for supporting them in this way. You need to balance the use of this excellent resource with the amount of time you are either allocated, or can give.

> **Typical uses**
> Primary: This dialogue tool gives an opportunity to discuss issues that have arisen during the day, but have not been followed up. For example, non-submission of homework, bullying, late arrival.
> Secondary: This is an excellent resource for individualised learning and development and fits very well into *Every Child Matters*. It can be used for pupils to raise confidential and personal matters that relate to PSHE and citizenship. It can also be used to provide additional support for a pupil who is struggling in class, or for whom English is a second language.

Attendance

This feature allows monitoring of pupil attendance on a group-by-group basis. Some systems may link to your school's pupil information system. It may not be appropriate to use in some schools which may use other electronic systems.

However, there are definite benefits to setting up and using this system. Late arrivals can be recorded as well as non-attendance. The system then allows you to print reports and isolate patterns in attendance and lateness. These can be very useful when reporting to parents, and also when justifying your end-of-year results.

This object is most useful when completed by all teachers and can build up a full picture of individual pupils, thereby proving very useful for those with pastoral responsibility.

Attendance reports may be combined with assessment and assignment reports to generate a more complete picture of the student. But, as with any form of attendance monitoring, it is only useful when completed consistently.

Typical uses
This feature can be used across primary and secondary schools to monitor and report on the attendance and lateness of all pupils.

'My files' area

This type of learning object typically behaves as would a local drive on the pupil's PC, with the advantage that the files are available from wherever the pupil can log on to the VLE. Most systems allow some form of control over permissions to the files, so that pupils could allow others access to files they wish to be made available to certain groups of users.

Typical uses
Primary: The 'My files' area can be used to store and share work for future use; it facilitates sharing of group work.
Secondary: Pupils can store files which need to be accessed from both school and home, enabling continuity for course work and homework; folders can be shared for group work.

Chat rooms

Most pupils are familiar with the use of chat rooms on the internet. Most VLEs have the facility to add chat rooms at your discretion. These can be used to offer a synchronous tutorial on a one-to-one or one-to-many basis as part of a distance learning programme. They can also be used as purely social forums, where chat may not be related at all to any academic work. This has the advantage that it encourages pupils to use the VLE. Another use is between primary and secondary schools as a 'buddying' facility to support Year 6 pupils in their transition to Year 7.

This can be an excellent use of the VLE. It encourages use between different age groups and can be used beneficially in a vertical 'house system' or tutor group system. You can set up a chat facility for pastoral discussions outside of courses, and you can also set up 'hobby' chat rooms.

Typical uses
Primary: Chat can help in providing a 'buddy' support facility with secondary school pupils. It can help to develop chat skills and enable pupils to discuss concerns, or chat about their hobbies to each other.
Secondary: It can enable pupils to support each other with homework and course work as well as providing a safe environment for them to chat to each other.

Instant messaging

Some VLEs are starting to offer an instant messaging option to allow synchronous one-to-one conversation between participants. It works in the same way as other messaging systems in that online users are visible and synchronous chat can be initiated immediately. Groups of users can be created to add to 'favourites' or 'ignore' lists. This object needs to be used carefully because of the amount of time pupils can waste on it both within lessons and outside school. If you do decide to use it you will need to prepare your pupils so that they understand the code of conduct for acceptable use and what will/will not be tolerated.

Typical uses
Primary: To inform about safe use of the internet and help pupils to develop the use of chat within a safe environment.
Secondary: Messaging can allow communication during group work.

RESEARCH SUMMARY RESEARCH SUMMARY **RESEARCH SUMMARY** RESEARCH SUMMARY

There are various models of teaching and learning. At the moment, research is ongoing into how these models fit into a VLE-based pedagogy. You are advised to look at electronic journals available via the internet or via your university library for current research. However, we would recommend that you read Von Brevern (2004), who challenges the reader to consider current models of teaching and learning styles. John Konrad's paper (2003) takes this discussion further. He applies the pedagogy of learning through the VLE in a higher education setting, but the implications he discusses can be applied to the school-based environment.

With regard to pedagogy, you will be aware of the importance of considering the different learning styles in your classroom. Lee et al (2005) examine the way that learners' cognitive style affects their information-processing habits. The findings in this article can be applied to school-based VLEs. Heinrich (2004) and Ulicsak (2004) highlight the importance of assessment for learning and peer assessment in electronically marked work. Johnson and Green (2004) explore the differences in method and performance of students undergoing assessment on screen and on paper.

CHAPTER SUMMARY

This chapter is concerned with developing your knowledge and awareness of some of the key objects that can be used to support your teaching. We have provided examples of the advantages and disadvantages for you to consider when selecting the objects most appropriate to your teaching.

A case study has been included for you to identify how a VLE has been used in practice, and to enable you to identify common aspects with your situation.

By working through the practical tasks, you will have created a collection of learning objects which address different teaching and learning styles for use in your professional role, underpinned by appropriate pedagogy.

What next?

This chapter has discussed a range of VLE objects, with many more being available. As a newly qualified teacher, it is important to be aware of a range of objects and to identify where they can enhance the teaching and learning in your subject area. Our advice is to start small: identify a series of objects that can be used with one area of theory with one group; develop and implement this and then evaluate it with your group before you go further. Practical advice would be to then develop an action plan to further develop your VLE across your teaching.

As a newly trained teacher, you will probably have a greater awareness of the use of VLEs than your colleagues. It would be good practice to share your knowledge and the developments you are working on with other staff and ask for their input.

Useful websites

www.becta.org.uk – British Educational Communications and Technology Agency – contains a wealth of advice and research regarding VLEs and ICT in schools.

www.everychildmatters.gov.uk – a government site dedicated to providing information and resources for the *Every Child Matters* agenda.

www.jisc.ac.uk – The Joint Information Systems Committee – a site aimed at supporting the use of ICT in further and higher education, which has a great deal of useful information about VLEs and their use.

www.moodle.org – the official site of the open-source Moodle VLE. The practicalities of using all the above learning objects are discussed on the forums here.

REFERENCES REFERENCES **REFERENCES** REFERENCES **REFERENCES** REFERENCES

Black, P and Wiliam, D (1998) *Inside the black box.* London: King's College,

Heinrich, E (2004) Electronic repositories of marked student work and their contributions to formative evaluation, *Educational Technology and Society*, 7 (3), 82–96.

Johnson, M and Green, S (2004) On-line assessment: the impact of mode on student performance. Paper presented at the British Educational Research Association Annual Conference, University of Manchester, 16-18 September 2004.

Konrad, J (2003) Review of educational research on virtual learning environments (VLE) – implications for the improvement of teaching and learning and access to formal learning in Europe. Paper presented at the European Conference on Educational Research, University of Hamburg, 17-20 September 2003.

Lee, C H M et al (2005) What affects student cognitive style in the development of hypermedia learning systems?, *Computers and Education*, 45 (1), 1–19.

Ulicsak, M H (2004) 'How did it know we weren't talking?': An investigation into the impact of self-assessments and feedback in a group activity, *Journal of Computer Assisted Learning*, 20, 205–211.

Von Brevern, H (2004) Cognitive and logical rationales for e-learning objects, *Educational Technology and Society*, 7 (4), 2–25.

FURTHER READING   FURTHER READING   **FURTHER READING**   FURTHER READING

Educators from many countries and all phases of education, ranging from novices to expert VLE users, share experiences and vision for VLEs. Extensive discussions on technical and pedagogical aspects of all learning objects can be found at **www.moodle.org**, membership of which is free.

4
Talk, chat and discussion – communications in virtual learning

By the end of this chapter you should be able to:

- understand and apply the different types of VLE tools available for teaching and learning in face-to-face and online situations;
- construct a realistic, pedagogical framework for your particular use of a VLE in school teaching;
- use a VLE to promote a sense of community online for pupils in schools, and use collaborative online networking tools to assist with this;
- differentiate between synchronous and asynchronous tools within the VLE, and be aware of the different ways that they can be deployed for effective use in schools;
- utilise the VLE technology within the classroom situation and demonstrate best practice for cascading this within schools.

This chapter addresses the following Professional Standards for QTS:
Q2, Q10, Q12, Q18, Q19, Q26

Introduction

Successful online learning is arguably independent of the VLE or particular software application that is used to support it. These provide the means to the end, but without an online community to drive the VLE, it can be likened to having a car without an engine – it just will not go, and no matter how many functions, buttons, bells and whistles it might have, if no one is motivated to use them, they may as well not be there. It is the intention, therefore, of this chapter to offer practical advice on how that community of learners may be created, and in doing so, recommend a minimum pedagogical framework for the successful use of VLEs for teaching and learning in schools. The VLE is seen as an enhancer of, providing further opportunities and alternatives, rather than as a replacement or substitute for, face-to-face classroom teaching and learning.

This chapter examines in detail a basic minimum pedagogical framework, with examples of how it can be used effectively for the implementation of VLEs in schools. The use of collaborative online group work is also described as a practical tool for the promotion of online community. Lastly, there is a brief overview of the use of both synchronous and asynchronous tools for teaching and learning in schools.

A pedagogical framework for the use of VLEs in schools

Figure 4.1 illustrates the main features of the pedagogical framework recommended for the use of VLEs for teaching and learning in schools.

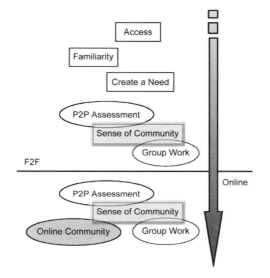

Figure 4.1 A minimum pedagogical framework for the implementation of VLEs for teaching and learning in schools

In this section, each of these features is described in detail, giving examples of how they might be applied in realistic situations, and also with some ideas of how effective each might be in cases where they have been previously tried and tested.

The VLE site needs to be available for pupils right from the start of their course, and should be introduced into classroom sessions as soon as possible. A familiarisation session illustrating the different facilities available to the pupils at the start of the course ensures that they are able to appreciate the usefulness of the VLE to them. Embed the use of the VLE in the face-to-face classroom sessions; for example, use it to access course information and to link to other useful websites as part of normal classroom sessions.

Teaching and learning using talk, chat and discussion

On teaching practice, you should encourage your pupils to become a face-to-face learning community. There are a number of ways in which this can be done, and often these depend on your actual teaching style. Typically, this would include the use of peer-to-peer assessment in class, whole-class discussion and brainstorming, and also collaborative group exercises to build their confidence in, and respect for, each other.

PRACTICAL TASK PRACTICAL TASK PRACTICAL TASK PRACTICAL TASK PRACTICAL TASK

For example, you could get your pupils to write a short essay (500–1,000 words) on their hobbies, giving them both the assessment and the marking criteria. You could then get them to swap their essays with a partner and mark each other's work. This could be done early on in your placement as a way of building up the mutual trust and respect within the group that is essential for the creation of any learning community. It is this which is arguably pivotal to the success of an online learning community. Without the support of peers and teachers, the community is unlikely to sustain itself. The skill of the teacher lies in being able to transfer any sense of community that has been created during face-to-face sessions into the online arena, by creating a need for the community independent of the place or space in which it might exist. If some or all of the face-to-face classroom situations of teaching and learning in schools can be transferred, then the mutual support experienced in class may continue online, that is, beyond the school gates.

Checklist
- Introduce the VLE into your classroom sessions right from the start.
- Embed the use of the VLE in your classroom sessions.
- Set peer-to-peer assessment exercises for your class.
- Build in group work and whole-group brainstorming into the classroom sessions.
- Set collaborative project work for your pupils to do in groups.

It is important to be authentic with pupils right from the start of the course. In order to gain their trust and respect, these also have to be given to them, and this may entail giving away part of yourself during class time, and encouraging them to do the same. This is done in order to engender the spirit of mutual trust and respect required for a sense of community to develop among the pupils, the idea being to create a rapport with your class that is unique to you, and which can exist independent of the medium in which it was first created.

Your presence in class is with you right from the start of your teacher training. So, whatever your presence is in class in face-to-face situations, you have to be able to transfer this to online situations. Having an overemphasised presence in face-to-face classroom situations is one way to make sure that, even if only some of this presence is transferred to online, then there is enough to give pupils the impression that the teacher is there independent of the place or space. If you are informal and make jokes in class, then keep these traits online. If you maintain order in class throughout whole-group discussion, then do this for online synchronous chat sessions. By all means adapt for being online, but retain your authenticity – the parts that make you the teacher that they have come to know and trust during your placement there. Using group work, small groups, large groups, pairs and so on to produce ideas, giving presentations, offering arguments, stimulating discussions and so on are all ways in which this can be achieved. Further information on blended learning can be found in Chapter 2.

In addition, it may also be possible to isolate key players in the group, those students who are more assertive and confident from the beginning, and are unafraid to ask questions or to make comments. You may be able to build on this to bring the rest of the class into line with them, for example, possibly by making a joke of the fact that they are always the ones to speak, or by letting the rest know that you will be asking anyone but them to speak next time. This somewhat informal type of teaching allows the others to become more relaxed in front of each other, and thus become more confident in speaking themselves. It initiates one of the processes by which a sense of community starts to form.

REFLECTIVE TASK

What did you learn about your pupils as they formed a learning community?

What did you learn about yourself as a trainee teacher as you deployed strategies to form the learning community?

Are there ways in which you could have formed the learning community better?

You should make the site the focus of communications with the group, creating a real need for it. Unless the VLE is the main means of communication for the group, especially when they are not in school, and is seen to be the place (or space) where they give and receive mutual collaborative support and help, it can quickly become peripheral to their needs. Encouraging the use of the VLE for information exchange, asking questions, sharing experiences, making social arrangements and so on, right from the start of the course, ensures that they are so used to relying on it to meet their needs that they continue to use it to do so in and out of school. Further information on how to blend the teaching and learning can be found in Chapter 2. In order to achieve this, you may also have to adapt your way of working – in the short term at least – to ensure that the community has the best possible chance to form.

Typical uses

Primary and secondary: Uploading presentations, references, timetables, articles and so on, to the VLE rather than using handouts, for example, as a means of making documents available. Using the announcements function in the VLE as a means of whole-group communications. Answering queries via discussion boards, and participating in the threads that pupils instigate, rather than setting up specific face-to-face workshops or group tutorials or seminars.

Once pupils get into the habit of contacting each other via the VLE, and can rely on it, particularly for issues that require help from more than one person at a time, then they are more likely to continue to do so. For example, they may raise a question and put it up on a discussion board for answers from the whole group to generate multiple ideas or discussions.

PRACTICAL TASK PRACTICAL TASK PRACTICAL TASK PRACTICAL TASK PRACTICAL TASK

Communicate with your group via the VLE, for example, for setting homework, for class discussions, for deadlines and so on.

You should try to provide online peer-to-peer collaboration exercises that can only be done via the VLE. In addition to the ideas proposed later in this chapter for collaborative online group work, the following examples may also be used to encourage online networked group learning among pupils.

- Get the pupils to produce a project plan for work towards an assignment deadline, or a revision schedule for their exams.
- Another very relevant and appropriate exercise is to get the pupils to collaborate to produce a small newspaper or poster to graphically illustrate the work they are doing in class.

CASE STUDY CASE STUDY CASE STUDY CASE STUDY CASE STUDY CASE STUDY

Communications in virtual learning

In a Year 12 ICT group in a large urban high school, the teacher had set up a message board facility (www.ssclc-forum.org.uk) and a web log (www.elgg.net/) where students could upload work, produce e-portfolios and peer-assess each other's work.

In all cases, no matter what the actual task is, the purpose of it is to require pupils to use the VLE, and in doing so add to the above list through which the need for it is created. Having to use it in this way for a specific purpose may also result in them seeing it as a regular part of their commitment to their course.

A critical mass of active participants

This is vital to the success of this type of online learning and participation. The most crucial aspect for the success of the VLE is the number of participating pupils. Even if all the ideas described above have been successfully created and implemented, without a critical mass of students to participate and interact online, the potential benefits of the VLE to the pupils will be lost – or simply just not gained.

One of the reasons for this is simply the initial class size. For example, in a class of 10 pupils or fewer, the chances of success might potentially be reduced dramatically. If, for example, only 50 per cent of that small group decide to use the VLE, and if 50 per cent of that participating group become discouraged by the small number of active participants, then that number may itself soon spiral downwards to zero. When the starting cohort is between 15 and 20, the chances of success increase dramatically.

Another thing to bear in mind is the level of ICT skills of pupils, and the level of their familiarity with the concept or use of VLEs, within each particular class. This may vary dramatically between groups and between different years, depending on their previous ICT experience in school.

For groups with lesser skills and knowledge of VLEs, you should adapt the access and familiarity sessions at the start of the course to ensure that all students reach a level at which they can comfortably access the VLE to meet their needs – before they are expected to use it outside school time. One way to do this is to take the class through the whole site, step by step, and to do this repeatedly as required, until students are comfortable with the system. Another way is to set pupils, as individuals or in groups, specific tasks to do on or using the VLE in class. These could be:

- using the VLE for research;
- navigating the site to look for particular information;
- testing the web links set up;
- initiating and reporting on threads in discussion boards.

The results of the tasks can then be presented to the rest of the class at a later session as a way to determine the level of understanding of the pupils with respect to the VLE. You could try this with different groups from the same year on your long placement.

Having said all that, even the best teacher in the world, with a brilliant VLE site, and a fabulous rapport with their pupils, may still fail to make this work. This is because certain pupils may choose never to take part in the online community. It just doesn't appeal to some people. Hopefully these are becoming rarer and will be a minority in any one class.

The advice here, for any teacher, would be not to give up. As stated previously, different years bring different cohorts, and any experienced teacher will know that what worked for one group may not work for another. When an online community takes off, the satisfaction in seeing it work, progress, and benefit those within it, in an almost synergistic way, far outweighs any negative experiences that may have been encountered along the way.

PRACTICAL TASK PRACTICAL TASK **PRACTICAL TASK** PRACTICAL TASK **PRACTICAL TASK**

Construct a detailed pedagogical framework for your groups in school to incorporate the teaching and learning strategies you are going to use with them.

Collaborative online group work

In order for pupils to get the most out of the VLE, it is essential, as stated previously, to create a need for it. Without this need, pupils may not participate in the various collaborative aspects offered by the VLE through the use of discussion boards and so on.

Typical uses

Primary and secondary: Giving pupils a mandatory group task that can only be done online is one way to ensure that all pupils participate in the VLE, and this type of task also has a threefold purpose:

1. It can create a need for the VLE and promotes collaborative networking and community between pupils.

2. It can enable them to experience first hand, and thus hopefully understand for themselves, how the VLE can be used to promote a sense of community online.

3. It enables them to appreciate how the VLE can be used for virtual collaborative group work, and thus apply it for use with their own course work and assignments.

One way to create an opportunity for online collaboration is to set group work for pupils that is to be done while they are on holiday, for presentation or review by the whole class and teacher when they next attend school. An example of one way to approach this is given here. The work must be set immediately prior to pupils leaving for holidays; for example, during their last class with you as a whole group, so that they have only minimal opportunity to collaborate face to face prior to the start of the holiday. You could do this on your long placement using either a half-term or full-term break over which to set the task. (Further examples of blended learning can be found in Chapter 2.)

In the example given here, the pupils are split into small groups for the purposes of the collaborative online assignment. The number and size of the groups depend on the number of the whole class, and it can often be useful to create the groups in such as way so as to encourage collaborative working between pupils who may not normally work together.

Each group is then required to collaborate via discussion boards to produce a fraction of an item, such as a project plan, or revision timetable, for example, for a specific part of their course(s), the idea being that when all the separate parts are added together, they make a complete, seamless product.

In this example, collaboration between the separate groups can only take place via a special 'liaison group' discussion board that only one member from each constituent group has access to. One way to set this up in the VLE is as follows. Pupils are assigned to a specific group created especially for the purposes of this assignment. This may be accessed via a 'Groups' button from the main screen in some systems.

Access to each group is restricted to the members of that particular group, and members within each group have permission to upload files, send emails and add messages to a discussion board, and so on, within the group. Individual group members can only access their own boards, thus ensuring that they can only collaborate within their own group.

In addition, a liaison group could be set up to 'oversee' the whole process. The main purpose of this group is to maintain communications between the other groups, so that the separate parts of the item being produced actually fit together as a whole. This group might consist of a representative member from each of the other groups, who meet on a separate liaison discussion board, to which only they have access, to discuss the progress of each separate group. It may also be useful to assign the role of 'project manager' for the exercise to one particular student. Their job would be to ensure that the liaison group was working effectively.

Ideally, the work set for this type of exercise should be practical and relevant to the course of study. Care must be taken to ensure that the end result is achievable in the time given, and that it is measurable in terms of outcomes and benefits to the students. One way to do this is to use the production of a necessary item, such as the project plan, or revision timetable example given above. This is something that is relevant to all pupils, and, given that each group only has to produce a small part of the end product, should not be too arduous a task for any single one of them.

Bear in mind that the main purpose of the exercise is to engender an online community while they are away from school, and to illustrate how a VLE could be used for this type of collaborative work for other parts of their course.

In terms of measurability, firstly, you are able to access all the groups, and while not participating in the boards (since this is an exercise for the pupils only) you are able to view the boards and consequently determine who is participating in the online collaboration. You are also able to determine how individuals are participating, whether it be through simple short messages, or longer, more discursive messaging with documents uploaded for others to share.

In addition to this, the presentation or review of the final product of the assignment should be built into later school classes, giving pupils both a deadline and a purpose to the exercise. This review might include the following.

- **Accessing the VLE to examine the amount and type of activity on the individual group boards.**
- **Presentation of the final product to the whole class and an analysis of its fitness for purpose.**

- Evaluating the exercise with the whole class in terms of the intended benefits to the pupils as outlined previously. Questions to be asked here include whether or not they found it useful as a means to understand VLEs; did they find it easy to collaborate online; and will they use this type of activity in their own future learning?

PRACTICAL TASK PRACTICAL TASK **PRACTICAL TASK** PRACTICAL TASK **PRACTICAL TASK**

Construct an exercise for the group that can only be done using the VLE.

Become a participant/observer for online networked learning.

REFLECTIVE TASK

How well did you feel the collaboration worked?

Would it work better with or without you?

Do you think your students benefited from the collaborative exercise and if so, how?

Synchronous and asynchronous communications technology for teaching and learning in schools

In this section, it is intended to describe, with examples, the use of some of the synchronous and asynchronous features of the VLE that can be used for teaching and learning in schools, while pupils are both in and out of school.

Synchronous tools

Within a VLE, it is possible to set up a prearranged time at which pupils can meet virtually, in real time, within the online space that is provided by the VLE. Having set up the time for the session (outside school hours and with parental permission) and having also informed the pupils of when and how to participate, each pupil would click on the 'Join' button to enter the virtual 'chat room'. In the chat room there would be others present, and some might join at various times during the session, the idea being that they could discuss topics related to their course outside school, with all their class mates, in real time. Pupils type in comments, questions and so on, and these can be seen by all participants as threads of conversations to which they can chose to respond or not.

You would normally set a time limit for each session, of, for example, one hour, and this might be at a time that was most convenient for the pupils (and parents) such as early evening, once they have returned home from school. This technology gives them an opportunity to 'meet up' with their peers in real time, and can facilitate the continuation of the community spirit that was present during face-to-face classroom sessions. It might be possible for you to arrange one or more of these types of sessions in your placements.

There are many advantages of using this type of technology to maintain a sense of community and mutual collaboration between pupils. Not least is the reduction in the sense of isolation that can be felt once they leave the school boundaries and are geographically separated from their peers.

The type of interactions that this synchronous session can provide for, with the facilitation of the teacher, include:

- **the different courses they are studying;**
- **their aspirations and plans for the future;**
- **their relationships with others in school;**
- **use of internet resources, and group work in lessons;**
- **sharing their thoughts on how they are coping with the course and the school assignments that they are required to produce.**

This list is not exhaustive, but it does give an idea of what the pupils are wanting to talk about – these are the things that are uppermost on their minds, their main worries and concerns. So, if the chat session is steered towards these types of subjects, then the pupils should get a great deal of benefit from participating in it. To this end, you should consider asking mainly open questions, and starting the discussion off with something that all pupils could comment on, such as how they are getting on with their course work, and so on. Depending on the sense of community within the group, pupils might also venture to ask questions regarding each other's well-being, and more personal questions concerning life beyond school.

One of the main advantages of this type of session that can be developed by you as the teacher is that it demonstrates, very visually (in that it is there as a list of conversation threads), what would be useful as discussion board topics. One way to progress the ideas presented in the synchronous chat session is to replicate them on the discussion boards. In this way, the benefits to the pupils from the synchronous session continue beyond that session throughout their course.

Typical uses

Discussion boards for particular popular threads from the synchronous session, such as relationships with teachers and other pupils, strategies for coping with assignments, workload and homework, plans for the future, resource sharing, and so on.

Instigate new threads on already populated boards to continue the lines of thought from the synchronous session. For example, on a board set up for assignments, you could start a new thread that further developed ideas from the synchronous session, or answered questions from that session in more detail.

Prior to embarking on this type of session, you should set out the 'house rules' for the session in terms of the type of language that is or is not acceptable, and whether or not personal issues are to be allowed, and so on. Pupils should also be informed if the session is to be recorded and archived for future use. Parental consent and access for all participants should be organised well in advance of any planned sessions.

There are a number of practical considerations to take into account when organising this type of activity for pupils.

- **Any technical difficulties with the access accounts or central server may result in not all pupils being able to access the session.**
- **There will never be a best, or most convenient, time for this type of live session, as it is not possible to please all pupils all the time. Thus having set up an initial session, the time slot should**

be reviewed and pupils asked about what times would be best for them. This should ensure that maximum participation is achieved.

- It should also be noted that the more participants there are, the harder the session is to facilitate, as each participant adds more comments to the screen. It is, of course, up to you to decide whether or not to participate with the pupils. You may chose to facilitate sessions at the start of the course, and then later on in the course, leave them to the pupils, preferring just to observe; or you may choose to participate actively in all sessions.
- One other thing to be aware of for this type of session is that of time lag – the gap between typing a message, and it being viewed on screen by other participants. This can lead to some mismatched, if interesting, threads. It can make the messaging appear disjointed and unsynchronised, particularly when an answer to one question appears after other questions have been asked. The time delay can affect the flow of text to such an extent at times that it resembles a 'Two Ronnies' sketch! This can lead to problems for you when you are trying to facilitate the discussion between participants and between the participants and themselves.

PRACTICAL TASK PRACTICAL TASK **PRACTICAL TASK** PRACTICAL TASK **PRACTICAL TASK**

Set up a synchronous session for your group(s).

After the session, talk to the whole class about the session and see if there are any issues from the session they would like to explore further.

Independent of how well the session is set up – and this applies to face-to-face as well as online sessions – some participants will get more out of it than others. Some pupils will prefer not to participate at all, as they may prefer more one-to-one communication with peers and the teacher. Even if only a small number participate and get something out of the session, it is worthwhile doing. Having this type of synchronous session, while possibly not as good as face-to-face classroom interactions for some, is better than nothing at all for most pupils. It gives them real-time access to each other on a grander scale than can be achieved through email or texting alone during times when they are not in school.

REFLECTIVE TASK

Did you feel the synchronous session went well?

How might you do it differently next time?

Asynchronous tools

In this section, the use of discussion boards (or forums) is explored as a means for asynchronous communication and collaboration between students.

Discussion boards within a VLE provide a very simple and effective means by which pupils can communicate with each other to share ideas and experiences, at a time when it is convenient for them. Discussion boards are 24/7 – they can be accessed at any time, and generally from anywhere (over the internet). They also provide an added advantage of being able to be read only, that is, unlike synchronous tools such as the chat session previously described, those students wishing to take advantage of the information exchange of the boards can do so without having any pressure to participate themselves.

Discussion boards may be accessed from the home screen for the site via the 'Discussion board' or 'Forum' button. Any number of discussion boards can be set up; however, it should be borne in mind that the more boards there are, for a limited number of pupils, the more likely it is that the messaging will become diluted. A typical post-16 class in a large secondary school is likely to have between 5 and 20 pupils – depending on the subject. In addition to this, not all students will choose to participate, and so, if there are endless boards to add messages to, and only a limited number of active messengers, the boards run the risk of being underused. Once pupils see that they are not being used, then the chances of any new messengers adding to them decreases significantly (Hramiak, 2006). Having a few, highly relevant boards is probably the best way to increase the chances of success of this feature of the VLE, and thus increase the benefits to the students.

CASE STUDY CASE STUDY CASE STUDY CASE STUDY CASE STUDY CASE STUDY

The use of interactive web facilities

Many schools take advantage of the facilities offered by the BBC website for revision purposes (*www.bbc.co.uk/bitesize*). The site provides revision materials, interactive ways to revise at all key stages, advice on planning and also a virtual area called 'Onion Street' where students can get help with their school work by talking to people their own age. They can also read and watch interviews with experts, and get advice on revision techniques and dealing with school stress.

Discussion boards as asynchronous discussion tools

Although somewhat obvious, the more the pupils use the discussion boards, the more they get out of them. It is advisable, therefore, to set up boards that are particularly pertinent to the way that the course progresses. These could reflect the face-to-face classroom sessions, or build on them to augment specific school sessions. Some tried-and-tested ideas for boards where pupils can share experiences and ideas specific to their course are as follows:

- **A discussion board for specific pieces of course work, for example. This could be set up to reflect the deadlines for the work, so that the messaging is pertinent to the work being undertaken at that particular time.**
- **A discussion board for help with assignments, or boards for each specific assignment or type of assignment. As with the course work boards, these could also be set up to run for times that reflect assignment hand-in dates, or set up to run with general issues on assignments for the duration of the course.**
- **A general issues, or social discussion, board.**

As the academic year progresses, it is useful to maintain the discussion boards in parallel with the progress of the students on the course. For example, the board relating to the first assignment could be removed (or archived) after students move onto their second assignment, and a board added at the appropriate time for UCCAS applications, for example, or for exams revision, as the course and year move on.

PRACTICAL TASK PRACTICAL TASK PRACTICAL TASK PRACTICAL TASK PRACTICAL TASK

Set up a series of discussion boards for your pupils and change them as you move through the academic year.

Set yourself up as the virtual revision expert for your pupils, using the discussion boards as a place where they can come to you for advice and help with revision.

As with the synchronous session, it is up to you whether or not you feel you should participate in the boards, or whether you should just observe the messaging within them. If the intention is to try to replicate on the boards, as far as possible, the sense of community with the class you achieved during classroom sessions, then you would generally join in to a lesser or greater extent with the messaging. You would become a part of the online classroom community in much the same way as you were part of the face-to-face classroom community, thus transferring your presence (from teacher to e-teacher) to the online situation as far as possible.

The boards are there to encourage pupils to share their experiences and collaborate in and out of school. This can take many forms, and, if the community that existed in face-to-face classroom sessions is successfully transferred to an online situation such as this, the boards can be literally 'swamped' with good ideas, help and assistance, shared experiences and thoughts in relation to both their school (and possibly private) lives. You can find more information on blended learning in Chapter 2.

RESEARCH SUMMARY RESEARCH SUMMARY RESEARCH SUMMARY RESEARCH SUMMARY

The practical suggestions for the use of a VLE described in this chapter show that there are ways in which technology can be used to enhance the teaching and learning in schools. The pedagogical framework describes a number of ways to establish a community of practice (Wenger, 1998) that can be successfully transferred from face-to-face to online situations. Pupils receive familiarisation sessions on the use of the VLE, and are given much group work in class, in order to get them working together as a learning community (Rovaii, 2001).

Previous research recommends that pupils have equal access to the shared electronic resources, and that a sense of community is created between the learners in the group, giving them the opportunity to structure the online experience for themselves. Research that has explored the 'connectedness' of the students who engaged with the VLE for the purposes of study, reports that there is a heightened sense of feeling connected as part of a wider learning community (Thurston, 2005). The forming of the sense of community is deemed to be a necessary initial step in online collaborative learning (Wegerif, 1998).

CHAPTER SUMMARY

The VLE for use in school teaching has to be fit for purpose. It is not all things to all people.

What is required from using a VLE for teaching in schools is a clear definition and description of the purpose, rationale and benefits of its use, prior to actually using it, in order to ensure that pupils are getting the most out of it.

A framework for the implementation of VLEs for this purpose was described in detail, giving examples of how each stage of the framework might be achieved.

What next?

From here you could adapt your teaching practices and strategies within the VLE and through the use of ICT, to move towards a greater use of online interactive and community-building techniques within your teaching.

Useful websites

www.contentgenerator.net/
Allows you to make your own interactive quizzes.
www.puzzlemaker.com
Use this to create word searches/cryptograms for starter activities, for example.
www.thekjs.essex.sch.uk/yates/index.html
This site contains lots of information on Key Stage 3 upwards for ICT resources.

REFERENCES REFERENCES **REFERENCES** REFERENCES REFERENCES REFERENCES

Hramiak, A J (2006) A pedagogical framework for the use of Information Technology in Initial Teacher Training. The 6th IEEE International Conference on Advanced Learning Technologies (ICALT), Kerkade, The Netherlands, 3–5 July 2000.

Rovaii, A P (2001) Building classroom community at a distance: A case study, *Educational Technology Research and Development,* 49, 33–48.

Thurston, A (2005) Building online learning communities, *Technology Pedagogy and Education,* 14, 353.

Wegerif, R (1998) The social dimension of asynchronous learning networks, *JALN,* 2.

Wenger, E (1998) *Communities of practice.* Cambridge, Cambridge University Press.

FURTHER READING FURTHER READING **FURTHER READING** FURTHER READING

Mehanna, W N (2004) e-Pedagogy: the pedagogies of e-learning, *ALT-J Research in Learning Technologies,* 12, 279–293.

Sloman, M (2002) *The e-learning revolution from propositions to action.* London: CIPD.

5
Electronic portfolios – outcomes for virtual learning

By the end of this chapter you should be able to:

- **know about the theory behind electronic portfolios with a focus on their use in teaching and learning;**
- **focus practically on how learning can be assessed through electronic portfolios;**
- **understand how electronic portfolios are designed to promote different types of learning;**
- **understand how the individual component parts of an electronic portfolio can be used in different contexts;**
- **know what electronic portfolios might look like in different contexts;**
- **identify the possible uses of an electronic portfolio in teaching, learning and assessment;**
- **plan, teach and assess using an electronic portfolio as an integral part of teaching, learning and assessment, in both primary and secondary phases.**

This chapter addresses the following Professional Standards for QTS:
Q4, Q8, Q10, Q12, Q14, Q17, Q23, Q25, Q27, Q28

Introduction

What is an electronic portfolio?

Collecting evidence of learning has always been a difficult issue for teachers, and trainee teachers might find they need to do this to provide evidence of what pupils have learned in their lessons as well as for the purposes of the school. This chapter examines the possibilities for recording learning and achievement using electronic media such as text, images, photography, digital video and hyperlinked presentations. These media, which are often combined and described as multimedia, are created using a range of programs, applications and devices on a computer. They can then be collected together and shared with you and the other teachers and pupils online in a VLE via a tool called an 'electronic portfolio' (e-portfolio).

As a teacher, you can provide images, texts, movies and other files for pupils to use in creating their work as well as give templates for pupils to use to guide their work. It is important to consider the different aspects that make up an e-portfolio as component parts which comprise a whole, rather than individual pieces of work. The whole principle of the e-portfolio is that it's the combination of work, the mixture of media and the ways in which it was assembled that is more important than individual finished products. In addition, because you and your colleagues can access files saved within the e-portfolio at any time, you can monitor the progress and development of pupils' work.

Examples of e-portfolio types

The principal benefit of using e-portfolios in the primary phase is that they can be used to support pupils to communicate through multimedia. This is particularly helpful with primary phase pupils who may still find using a keyboard or writing lots of text difficult. In addition, the ability to use images, sounds and text in the work they produce enables pupils to express their ideas more creatively. Examples of simple multimedia projects which can be created and shared via a VLE might include the following.

- **Literacy – pupils using a familiar story such as in literacy hour can make an audio recording of themselves reading it. This reading could be accompanied with an electronic book made by simple hyperlinking of word-processing pages. This could be shared with younger pupils via the VLE.**
- **Numeracy – mathematical puzzles can often be most easily explained visually. Simple problems and puzzles can be explained using annotated drawings or photos. Teachers can look at the results and give feedback via the VLE.**
- **History-based topic – simple web-quests, where teachers set some questions to be answered or information to be found. This can support independent learning using carefully selected sites on the internet. Questions and websites can be posted on the VLE.**
- **Art – there are a number of copyright-free image sites on the web which can be posted on the VLE for pupils to use and view (try *www.scran.ac.uk*). Pupils might choose from a selection to illustrate a particular genre or theme – for instance, ways in which animals are portrayed – and use this to compose their own work.**

There are a number of skills that pupils need to acquire in order to create and publish multimedia work. However, recent developments in hardware and software mean that creating and editing images, sounds and text is simple enough for primary age pupils to master. E-portfolios in VLEs provide a place to keep these resources and for the teacher to review work in progress. In addition, if pupils can work online they can collaborate on tasks.

While on professional teaching practice placement in schools, you can choose one of these projects to fit in with what you are teaching. It is better to concentrate your efforts on one subject area or topic rather than trying to introduce e-portfolios in all areas of your teaching.

The principal benefit of using e-portfolios in the secondary phase is that they enable pupils to communicate their ideas through multimedia. Where pupils are working on course work for examinations, collecting and developing this kind of work via the VLE as an e-portfolio enables teachers to monitor progress and pupils to keep work safe and neat as it develops. Trainee teachers in the secondary phase might find it difficult to establish such practices on short school placements. However, as practice for your future career it would be useful to try multimedia approaches to creating work.

- **Science – video and digital photos are increasingly a useful resource for pupils studying habitats and other natural phenomena. Over a period of time the study of a particular place can be supported by creating an e-portfolio which is added to over several weeks or months, building up a picture of patterns and changes over time. In addition, this resource kept online is available for teachers to monitor progress.**

- **English** – pupils can use existing online resources such as RM's Living Library to find resources about genres such as drama or poetry. These resources might be in the form of websites, photos or text. These can be collated using an e-portfolio along with pupils' reflections.
- **Modern foreign languages (MFL)** – finding and using websites which are appropriate to the level of language learners is difficult. Teachers of MFL can use a VLE to collect suitable sites and make them available to learners. Pupils can then work on these sites regularly in projects, for example, a regular word-processed summary of news stories from international news sites can be written and posted to the pupils' area of the VLE for the teacher to comment on.

As pupils come into secondary education with increasingly advanced ICT skills learned in the primary phase, teacher are able to take advantage of this, as well as increasing access to ICT resources in secondary schools to use ICT in teaching and learning. Studies such as *The big pICTure* (DfES, 2003) have shown that ICT is motivational for pupils, and where pupils need encouragement with collecting and developing resources for course work and other projects, the use of e-portfolios and other VLE tools can be very useful.

> **PRACTICAL TASK** PRACTICAL TASK **PRACTICAL TASK** PRACTICAL TASK **PRACTICAL TASK**
>
> Consider how an e-portfolio could be used on your next professional teaching practice placement in school. Try to experiment using a small area of the curriculum or one class or group at first.

Rationale and advantages of using e-portfolios

Creativity

The definition of creativity from the National Curriculum in Action Creativity website is broad:

> *First, they [the characteristics of creativity] always involve thinking or behaving* **imaginatively***. Second, overall this imaginative activity is purposeful: that is, it is directed to achieving an objective. Third, these processes must generate something* **original***. Fourth, the outcome must be of* **value** *in relation to the objective.*
> (DfES, 2005)

- **E-portfolios can promote imaginative work** from pupils because they encourage the use of a variety of media which can help pupils express their ideas in imaginative ways.
- **Creating e-portfolios helps pupils work purposefully** because the results are both tangible and can be shared and published in a variety of ways. The ability to share electronically created resources with peers (via email or VLE discussion boards or file sharing) is very motivational for pupils.
- **Work created using a variety of media** brought together in an e-portfolio gives pupils opportunities to create original work through bringing together a variety of media, because the best portfolios build up gradually and can demonstrate how work has progressed. This should help teachers and pupils evaluate work as it progresses and help teachers encourage pupils to follow their own ideas.
- **E-portfolios can help pupils create work of value** if the portfolios are part of a meaningful system of assessment. Formative assessments of pupils' work can support course work and project work as it progresses. If electronically created media are acceptable for course work, this also helps pupils

feel their work is valued. In addition, the presentational benefits of creating work using ICT can help pupils produce work of which they are proud.

There are many creative uses of e-portfolios. However, all this comes with a 'health warning' for teachers about working with students to create multimedia work. Pupils can get very distracted by the range of tools which many multimedia packages offer. For example, when working with digital photos they can be re-coloured; size, shape, and orientation can be changed; and photos can be added to with text or images altered. This range of possibilities can be distracting for pupils who might want to 'play' with the tools rather than focus on the task in hand. For this reason teachers must be very well focused on their objectives for the session/activity and what they want pupils to achieve. It is also important for teachers to be clear about allowable timescales. This should help pupils make the best of the opportunities while working towards the objectives in a focused way.

While on teaching practice, it is sometimes difficult to work effectively in ICT, with limited timescales to develop skills and activities, but this should not dissuade trainee teachers from working in this way on a small scale.

REFLECTIVE TASK

Consider how you promote creative learning in your teaching already. Could any of these ways have been supported or developed using e-portfolios, either for formal or informal support and feedback to pupils?

Motivation

The big pICTure report (DfES, 2003) collects together a range of recent research reports into ICT in schools. It is clear from the findings of the various reports that ICT is important to pupils' lives and that they find using it in their learning motivational.

> *There are some clear messages about the motivational potential of using ICT in teaching and learning, and the opportunities ICT affords for both engaging students directly and motivating an engagement in subject learning via ICT.* (DfES, 2003)

This raises an important point. Through using ICT in teaching, teachers can encourage enthusiasm for and pupil motivation in the subjects they are teaching. Although the current discussions about pupils having dominant 'learning styles' is controversial, most successful classroom practitioners recognise that variety in teaching approaches is good for them and for their pupils. Because the essence of an e-portfolio is that it contains a variety of work, this approach to students collating work and teacher assessment is positive and productive.

However, teachers must remain focused on the subject objectives of what they are teaching rather than allowing the style of using e-portfolios to take over from the substance of their content. As a trainee teacher on placement in a school, it is sometimes difficult to 'keep all the plates spinning' – to teach effectively, to manage behaviour, to assess pupils' learning, to be interesting and interactive. However, you should be positive about the benefits of using ICT effectively in these ways and try to incorporate developments in your practice gradually.

PRACTICAL TASK PRACTICAL TASK **PRACTICAL TASK** PRACTICAL TASK **PRACTICAL TASK**

Identify pupils who lack motivation in their work. Consider the nature of this lack of motivation. Set up a small test group of pupils to trial e-portfolio work.

Inclusion

The inclusion agenda is one which no serving or trainee teacher can ignore. Its scope is substantial and the effect which it has on schools is wide ranging. In 2001 the Department for Education and Skills set out for schools what inclusion should encompass. These included:

Principles of an inclusive education service

- *With the right training, strategies and support nearly all children with special educational needs can be successfully included in mainstream education.*
- *Schools, local education authorities and others should actively seek to remove barriers to learning and participation.*
- *All children should have access to an appropriate education that affords them the opportunity to achieve their personal potential.* (DfES, 2001)

Although these principles do not directly mention ICT, it can make a substantial impact on including pupils who otherwise would encounter barriers to their full participation in education. E-portfolios containing multimedia work can support inclusion because ICT can enable learners to express their learning in ways which are accessible to them. There is a wide range of devices, hardware and software which have been designed to promote inclusion. These enable learners to overcome barriers to learning and should support pupils in creating work in multimedia. Some examples might include:

- **pupils with limited expressive language can record practical examples of work using video or digital photographs;**
- **pupils who are unable to use a keyboard easily can produce audio files of their ideas;**
- **pupils who find concentration difficult can produce a number of short pieces of work to address a question and collate them via the e-portfolio.**

Most importantly, e-portfolios allow teachers to monitor the progress of pupils' work, which supports teachers in meeting individual needs through their interventions at different points in the learning process.

Teachers must bear in mind that when using a range of electronic devices, hardware and software, some pupils are not able to participate due to physical or cognitive impairments. As with all issues relating to inclusion, there are no easy answers to what teachers should do to maximise inclusion in a diverse class. Each teacher must work with pupils and the school to manage inclusion issues. Support from an experienced teacher is essential in addressing these issues. However, e-portfolios of work can help support the inclusion of pupils in a number of ways.

REFLECTIVE TASK

REFLECTIVE TASK

Find out what tools and devices are available in your placement school to support students with barriers to learning and special needs of various kinds. How might these support students in the use of an e-portfolio as an assessment tool on your courses?

Collaboration

Collaboration and communication are key learning skills. Despite the fact that the current education system relies heavily on assessing the achievements of the individual, such skills are highly valued in the world of work and business in the twenty-first century. Writing in the year 2000 about the 'unfinished revolution' in education, the academic John Abbot sets out a radical vision for the future of education (Abbott and Ryan, 2000). Abbot and Ryan's book examines how education needs to change to meet the demands of the future. In an appendix to the book, Dr Stephanie Pace Marshall sets out her ideas about a future learning environments including that:

> *Collaboration, interdependence and internal rewards are more powerful motivators for learning.* (Abbott and Ryan, 2000, p261)

When changes are made in schools, teachers only really are fully committed to them if they can be convinced that the changes are in the best interests of their pupils. This healthy teacher scepticism has protected pupils from many fly-by-night innovations in the past. However, an increase in pupil-to-pupil collaboration in work is potentially very beneficial and teachers should work towards ways of teaching where collaboration is more a part of both learning and assessment. Collaboration can:

- **motivate pupils;**
- **enhance creative approaches;**
- **minimise misconceptions;**
- **encourage participation.**

E-portfolios can be set up on VLEs which can be accessed by one or more pupils and the teacher. An e-portfolio of multimedia work can support pupil-to-pupil collaboration through allowing pupils to share work in progress electronically, for example a mind map of a concept can be shared via the VLE with other pupils for additions and comments. Also pupils can work together on a project, for instance editing different bits of a video, and view each other's contributions using an e-portfolio.

Most teachers value face-to-face paired and group work in teaching sessions. However, there are a number of problems associated with this, including how to best group pupils and how to ensure all members of the group contribute appropriately. Because VLEs allow teachers to monitor electronically which pupils are using the systems and when, they can monitor contributions to some extent. However, teachers must exercise the same rules with electronic collaboration as they do with face-to-face collaboration and be aware of the signs which might indicate a pupil who may not be 'pulling their weight' in a given task.

Originality and plagiarism

One of the great things about the rise of electronic media is the potential to share things – information in text and pictures, music and video, etc. Broadband internet access has made sharing multimedia resources simpler than ever. However, this also has raised the issue of illegal and inappropriate copying of material. This is a matter of great concern for teachers, although the copying of work is not a new phenomenon in education. Teachers who are engaging in teaching and learning with pupils making multimedia resources to contribute to e-portfolios must have systems in place to make sure that work submitted by pupils as their own is that.

Rules and responsibilities of e-portfolios

In your position as a trainee in school, you may not have much control over these issues, but you need to find out how schools are dealing with them in terms of policy and practice.

As assessment methods develop and change, teachers need to make sure that the systems are fair and rigorous. Where e-portfolios are adopted by teachers, either as a method of course work assessment or in a less formal capacity, teachers must make sure that they have the right rules in place for pupils. These rules will obviously differ depending on the age of students and the uses to which the teacher puts the portfolios, but the following can be used as guidelines.

- **No material should be directly copied from the internet.**
- **Where information from the internet is used, it should be expressed in the pupils' own words and the reference given.**
- **Images used should either be made by pupils or taken from copyright-free sites and the source acknowledged.**
- **Collaboration between pupils on work is encouraged but should be with the knowledge of the teacher.**
- **Portfolios will be regularly checked by teachers.**
- **Communications tools associated with the e-portfolios available should only be used to communicate about work.**

Building e-portfolios into teaching and learning in the primary phase

First stages

Teachers must plan carefully when they are setting out to introduce e-portfolios to pupils in the primary phase. The best approach is to start with some simple tasks and uses, building up to complex tasks as pupils and teachers become confident. Having said this, challenge and excitement are important for pupils' motivation. Striking the balance will be the key to success and each teacher will make these decisions themselves. However, the following activities might be good to get pupils started.

Typical uses

In science pupils can take a series of digital photographs as an investigation progresses. These can be posted to the e-portfolio.

In English pupils can develop written work with the help of the teacher by uploading work for comment and developing it in response.

In maths pupils can work in pairs to develop presentations explaining how to solve problems and upload these to an e-portfolio for use by peers.

Many pupils will want to illustrate work using images. It is a good idea to develop their awareness of safe and legal ways to get images from the web. Teachers can provide files of images to use in the construction of portfolios, and pupils working collaboratively can build files of images as an introductory activity when starting a project. Wikipedia has a good selection of links to image resources at: **http://en.wikipedia.org/wiki/Public_domain_ image_resources**

These simple tasks can be developed by teachers into formative assessment tasks. However, at the early stages it is inadvisable to use e-portfolios for formal assessments and both pupils and teachers may lack confidence in using these media. Design is an important issue and this is discussed at length in Chapter 7.

Moving on

Once simple skills such as those described above have been developed, more complex activities can be worked on which put the accumulated skills together. In the activities outlined above, pupils will have learned to:

- **create and upload images to the portfolio;**
- **create and modify text;**
- **collaborate by sharing work with peers.**

Practical activities

These skills can be brought together in one activity – where pupils use a template from the teacher to build up an e-portfolio reflecting their ideas. For example, in a science topic on animals, pupils could gather ideas through web-quest devised by the teacher. These ideas could be in the form of '10 animal facts', supported by pictures. Alongside this pupils could visit a local habitat and record the number of animals seen in a spreadsheet which can by hyperlinked to the fact page, and supported with images or even video they create on the visit. In this way pupils have used a variety of media to demonstrate their learning, which will not only motivate them with a range of learning styles but also allows pupils to develop individual and creative work.

Figure 5.1 is an example of a simple e-portfolio which is being developed from uploaded files, which have been created by the teacher and pupils. On the left is the e-portfolio document itself; on the right, a library of images which are available, along with the tools for students to upload their own documents to the portfolio.

'Bells and whistles'

E-portfolios in VLEs can develop in a number of ways. At primary school level it is best to keep the technology and the processes of creating the contents of the portfolio simple and straightforward. However, primary pupils might benefit from using their work in a number of ways which could add value to projects.

Figure 5.1 Example of a simple e-portfolio for a topic on animals in Key Stage 2

PRACTICAL TASK PRACTICAL TASK **PRACTICAL TASK** PRACTICAL TASK **PRACTICAL TASK**

Start pupils on simple activities where they can share their work. Examine the impact on motivation as a result of trying:

- **publishing photos they have taken to the web;**

- **sharing a project with another school;**

- **developing learning materials such as books, videos or animations which can be shared with younger pupils.**

In this way you can make assessments of pupils' work, ICT skills and also their ability to share, communicate and co-operate. These diverse assessment opportunities add value to the learning.

Building e-portfolios into teaching and learning in the secondary phase

First stages

Assessment at secondary level is a topic which is much discussed at the moment. The Tomlinson report, and its fallout, have made teachers, schools and awarding bodies examine closely the process of formal public examinations at secondary level.

However, while this is going on, teachers still have to do the everyday work of assessment. Considering that electronic testing for ICT at Key Stage 3 will be introduced in 2008, it may be that electronic assessment will play an increasing role in formal assessment procedures in secondary schools. Teachers can prepare for this by beginning to integrate electronic methods of assessment into their teaching. This might mean that they use electronic testing (not covered in this chapter) but there are also many benefits to using e-portfolios with secondary phase pupils.

- **Use of ICT is motivational for pupils.**
- **Links between learning at home and school can be strengthened through VLEs.**
- **ICT can support pupils with a variety of abilities and learning styles and enables teachers to meet individual needs more effectively.**

Teachers in the secondary phase expect their pupils to have acquired some ICT skills in primary school. It is hoped that pupils will be able to use these skills from the beginning of the secondary phase to support their learning.

Typical uses

E-portfolios in the secondary phase can be used in different ways from those that they are likely to be used in the primary phase. One of the main uses would be for homework. The following homework tasks could form part of an e-portfolio of work for a subject:

- a multimedia write-up of a science experiment;
- the results of a history/art/geography web-quest;
- a piece of creative writing supported by photographs.

The results of a web-quest in a subject like history can be collated into a multimedia and hyperlinked document. This medium has advantages over print and paper-based results as it allows the teacher to explore the results immediately. Figure 5.2 shows a page about the links between the Cold War and the 'space race'. The pupil has attached the links used before going on to explain what he found out. Working in this way allows teachers to effectively assess the impact of a web-quest or research project on a particular pupil's learning in a straightforward way. Teachers might use this to go on to set additional tasks for pupils to meet their learning needs.

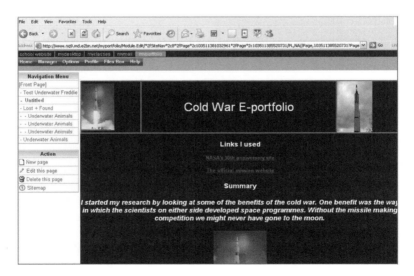

Figure 5.2 An example of a secondary phase web-quest for a history topic

Moving on

One significant difference between the primary and secondary phases of education is the organisation of learning into subject areas. As more primary schools return to cross-curricular topic work as a result of the Primary Strategy, benefits for learning are increasingly apparent. The current structure and nature of secondary education and the fact that is significantly influenced by the examinations system mean that opportunities for cross-curricular work are likely to be limited. However, as the examination system may at some point develop to reflect the more cross-curricular 'diploma' system advocated by the Tomlinson report, it may be that secondary phase teachers are able to use portfolios to work with colleagues in other subject areas.

REFLECTIVE TASK

Consider the cross-curricular links which might be possible with other subject areas. How might an e-portfolio support this? If possible, work with another trainee teacher in a different subject area.

'Bells and whistles'

Video and music are part of the culture of young people. If the power of these communication methods can be harnessed by teachers, there may be significant advantages for teaching and learning. The future of such technologies and assessment is likely to move in directions which haven't yet been mapped. Teachers wishing to be at the forefront of such developments should read NESTA Futurelab's paper on the future of digital technologies and reform of the 14–19 agenda, **www.nestafuturelab.org/research/reviews/reviews_13/ 13_01.htm**

Edited video files can become part of e-portfolios, as video can be uploaded to the VLE and links inserted into e-portfolio files.

PRACTICAL TASK PRACTICAL TASK PRACTICAL TASK PRACTICAL TASK PRACTICAL TASK

Find out how to access video recording equipment in your professional placement schools. There might be expertise in the school in using this, so find this out too. What experience have students had of making and using video in their learning?

RESEARCH SUMMARY RESEARCH SUMMARY RESEARCH SUMMARY RESEARCH SUMMARY

As with all areas in ICT, research into e-portfolios is developing rapidly. Academics and teachers are working together to address many pressing issues. As your career in education develops, it is important to keep an eye on progress in research in ICT. The following sites might be useful places to start, as they are well organised, comprehensive and reliable.

- NESTA Futurelab facilitates research into innovations in ICT in education. *www.nestafuturelab.org/index.htm*
- Becta (The British Education Communications and Technology Agency) works closely with government and other agencies to support ICT in schools. *www.becta.org.uk/*
- The *British Journal of Educational Technology* publishes its academic papers online. *www.blackwellpublishing.com/journal.asp?ref=0007-1013*

The potential of digital portfolios to meet the complex needs of education has been identified by NESTA Futurelab in their literature review on e-assessment:

> *An historical legacy which bedevils the current education system in the UK is the distinction between 'academic' and 'practical' subjects. This was enshrined in the 1944 Education Act, which created grammar, technical and secondary modern schools (Tattersall, 2003). Abstract thinking is important; appropriate action in context that rests on practical competence is important. Neither is much use on its own, and students should be taught to both abstract and apply. For this to become a classroom reality, assessment systems must require students to show the full spectrum of competencies in a number of school subjects. If high-stakes assessment systems fail to reward such behaviours, they are unlikely to be the focus of much work in school. E-portfolios offer a way forward.* (Ridgeway and McCusker, 2004)

As the education system undergoes change at both primary level, in favour of a more cross-curricular approach, and at secondary level towards a multi-disciplinary diploma, methods of assessment which allow pupils to compile a record of the full range of their achievements will become increasingly needed. A range of practical, collaborative, creative tasks can be collected together as an e-portfolio using a range of media which no other format will allow.

There have also been a number of small-scale research projects into e-portfolios. These have begun to develop the body of knowledge about how e-portfolios can support teaching, learning and assessment in a range of school contexts. At the time of writing, the majority of these are based in the USA. The research has shown that e-portfolios can be of use with students with special needs (Fine, 2001) because of the range of media (including photos and video) that can be used to express ideas. This is supported by research which looks at e-portfolios as an extension of paper portfolios, with all the benefits for learning this kind of assessment can bring in their ability to track student progress (Ahn, 2004). The benefits of the portfolio approach are seen not just as inclusive but also potentially creative. (Diehm, 2004)

There are also a number of projects which examine the use of e-portfolios in further and higher education contexts. Although the conclusions of these may only be partially applicable to school contexts, the more general ones may well be worth examining (Mason, Peglar et al, 2004).

CHAPTER SUMMARY

This chapter is about electronic learning portfolios. It defines them and sets them in the context of research about VLEs.

Effectively used, electronic learning portfolios can have a significant effect in four key areas: creativity, motivation, inclusion and collaboration.

The advantages and disadvantages of using electronic learning portfolios are examined in these areas.

Finally, examples and suggestions are given for the primary and secondary phases of possible uses of e-portfolios to collate pupils' work for assessment.

What next?

Although at the time of writing no use is made of e-portfolios in formal assessments (such as public exams or end of key stage testing), you should keep an eye out for pilot schemes and opportunities to promote electronic assessment of all kinds.

Useful websites

The NESTA Futurelab regularly updates with reports, advice for teachers and literature reviews. **www.nestafuturelab.org/index.htm**

REFERENCES REFERENCES **REFERENCES** REFERENCES **REFERENCES** REFERENCES

Abbott, J and Ryan, T (2000) *The unfinished revolution*. Stafford: Network Educational Press.

Ahn, J (2004) Electronic portfolios: Blending technology, accountability and assessment, *T H E Journal,* 31 (9), 12–18.

DfES (2001) *Inclusive schooling*. London: DfES.

DfES (2003) *The big pICTure: The impact of ICT on attainment, motivation and learning*. London: DfES.

DfES (2005) National Curriculum in Action website. **www.ncaction.org.uk/creativity/whatis.htm**

Diehm, C (2004) From worn-out to web-based, *Phi Delta Kappan*, 85 (10), 792–794.

Fine, L (2001) Special-needs gaps, *Education Week*, 20 (35), 26–30.

Mason, R, Peglar, C et al (2004) E-portfolios: an assessment tool for online courses, *British Journal of Educational Technology*, 35 (6), 717–727.

Ridgeway, J and McCusker, S (2004) *Literature review of e-assessment*. Bristol: NESTA.

FURTHER READING FURTHER READING **FURTHER READING** FURTHER READING

Ridgeway, J and McCusker, S (2004) *Literature review of e-assessment*. Bristol: NESTA. This short and well-written report will help you develop a wider understanding of the issues of students creating work and being assessed in electronic and multimedia formats.

6
Tasks, tests and feedback

By the end of this chapter you should be able to:

- design differentiated tasks which can be effectively delivered via a VLE;
- discuss good practice and the pitfalls of designing online tests;
- develop your skills in providing effective feedback to support learning using the VLE in a variety of contexts.

This chapter addresses the following Professional Standards for QTS:
Q4, Q8, Q10, Q12, Q19, Q22, Q23, Q24, Q25, Q26, Q27, Q28, Q30

Introduction

This chapter discusses a range of issues relating to the practical aspects of getting your teaching materials onto your VLE. It examines a range of matters that you need to consider when moving your lessons and assessment to the VLE. It also gives you practical help in using blended learning in the classroom. The first half links with Chapter 2, focusing on the different areas of the lesson: starter, episode(s) and plenary, and what steps to take to begin the process of using blended learning in practice. The second half looks at establishing good practice when assessing your pupils, and links to Chapter 3 by using a variety of the assessment objects discussed in that chapter.

Tasks

When planning your lessons it is important to plan a variety of tasks that are differentiated. In the same way, you need to ensure that you have differentiation when using the VLE to deliver your tasks. With the VLE this can be done in various ways. For the more able you need to think about increasing the level of challenge. You may prefer to set them a different task from the rest of the group that still supports the learning objectives/outcomes for the lesson. You may want to include elements of research that will stretch them further and provide scaffolding to higher-level skills. For the less able you may want to produce writing frames and simpler concepts, possibly supported by the use of more graphic images or less textual content.

For the different courses, groups or projects you teach, you may want to provide a range of links to different resources. You may also want to encourage the use of email support, either via peer groups that you set up or with yourself. With the VLE, you can also set up a variety of tasks and resources aimed at different levels, and enable the pupils to select which ones are appropriate to them. This helps them to develop as independent learners.

PRACTICAL TASK PRACTICAL TASK **PRACTICAL TASK** PRACTICAL TASK **PRACTICAL TASK**

Consider a small project or topic you are going to teach or have taught. Using a concept map, sketch out the existing tasks and identify how you can break them down for incorporation into the VLE. Which tasks can easily be transferred into the VLE? Would you need to develop additional tasks to support the use of the VLE in the project/topic? To extend this task, consider breaking the tasks into different learning objects (see Chapter 3) to ensure there are a variety of activities.

Remember that as with all groups you teach face to face, students using the VLE have different learning styles. The VLE is an excellent resource for providing learning opportunities for each learning style because such a wide range of media can be stored and made available to your pupils. If you are not familiar with the range of learning styles, you are advised to refer to the Teachernet web link listed at the end of this chapter; it provides a simple reference to the main learning style theories. It is very simple to link your VLE to learning style inventories that can help you to assess pupils' learning styles, such as the one at *www.acceleratedlearning.com/method/test_flash.html*

VLEs in non-traditional school settings

Some pupils prefer to learn from home and find the school environment difficult. There may also be pupils who are unable to attend school, for a variety of reasons. By planning tasks carefully, after considering their learning style and appropriate differentiation, you can really improve and develop their learning via the VLE. You might also have pupils who don't learn well in the morning, but are very happy to come home and log on to finish projects when they get home. Again, the tasks you put on the VLE can help them to develop their skills, knowledge and understanding. You might like to look at Professor Stephen Heppel's 'Not School' website to see an example of supporting these pupils in a different environment. If you are providing learning for pupils who work mainly from home, you need to make sure that tasks are adequately supported with online resources to complement the content delivered in the lesson. Also, ensure there is the potential for them to 'socialise' via the VLE with the rest of the group, as well as a link to your email for additional help and support.

REFLECTIVE TASK

Reflect back on a group you have taught recently. Consider the way your pupils learnt – using the VAK theory of learning styles, what would be the division of visual, auditory and kinaesthetic learners? Produce a table with the headings of Visual, Auditory and Kinaesthetic. Under each heading, write in the types of learning objects (see Chapter 3) which would address that particular learning style. You can use this information to choose learning objects suitable for your pupils.

When you are uploading your tasks it is important to ensure that they are accessible from home and school on as wide a variety of hardware as possible. This means you need to keep to standard file types, such as rich text format (rtf), jpeg images, mp3 audio, mpeg movies and html. Some proprietary formats such as MS Word are now supported by a wide variety of software and have become a *de facto* standard. While it is not ideal to use these, you can do so within your VLE if this is the main software the pupils have at home.

Virtual learning for students with English as an additional language

As part of your teaching standards you need to evidence teaching pupils for whom English is an additional language (EAL). You can make excellent use of your VLE to support these pupils. These pupils have different levels of language and will need support with terminology within your lessons. It is essential to provide them with as much support and help as possible to access your lesson and resources. One way of doing this is to provide links to an online translator. These can be found using a web search. Examples you might like to look at include **www.freetranslation.com** and **www.babelfish.altavista.com**

To provide additional support for your EAL pupils you can use peer translation. Forums and instant messaging can enable pupils of the same language, but with different abilities, to translate for each other in 'real time'. Different media can be used to illustrate complex concepts that are difficult to translate. For example, the use of screen-capture software can help to demonstrate how to use different aspects of software; audio can be used to support a demonstration with a variety of languages; screen shots can be used to show pupils with EAL how a final product should look; presentations can be accompanied by audio in different languages; and video capture can be used to demonstrate science experiments, etc., with audio files of different languages. You might want to look at Audacity software, which is open-source recording software available from Sourceforge – **http://audacity.sourceforge.net**

Certain VLEs allow the user to select the language that the VLE uses. This will not affect the language of the content, but the language of the VLE. This can be particularly useful, and an excellent tool for creating an enhanced learning environment for EAL pupils. It could be beneficial to your school to make links with schools abroad; the British Council website will provide you with help and support in doing this. You can contact them and state which country you would like to establish a link with at **www.britishcouncil.org** – you will need to link to their international portal. You can also find useful help and advice on teaching EAL students via **www.standards.dfes.gov.uk/keystage3/**, which has booklets for most subjects titled *'Access and engagement in [subject]'* – each of which contains a wealth of helpful advice. Another useful website is **www.literacytrust.org.uk**

Organisation and design

Chapter 7 deals with design issues in detail. It is important when thinking about your tasks to consider how to organise them before you start to upload them. You might want to put them in folders for different courses, projects, groups, etc., and within that you might want to consider breaking them down into weeks. This can help you when it comes to presenting them, and ensuring variety of activities on a week-by-week basis. You can also put them into topics that reflect your teaching units – see Figure 6.1. To aid pupil understanding you can use colour-coding; for example, you could code all the assignments in red, quizzes in blue, resources in green, etc.

As teachers, we are always aiming to develop our pupils into independent learners. One way of using the VLE to aid this is to use it for deadlines. For all key stages students need to meet deadlines. You can link your deadlines automatically to the calendar facility in the VLE (see Chapter 3). Many VLEs do this automatically and some systems can automatically remind students when they are nearing, or have missed, a deadline. By automating the deadlines and giving parents access to the VLE, parents can also be aware of imminent deadlines and add support and encouragement to their child to achieve. Teachers can also have deadlines that are independent of the tasks, e.g. homework deadlines, or reminders of work that needs doing before a task can be accessed by the pupils. If the whole school uses the calendar facility it becomes easier to balance the workload; this can be particularly useful at Key Stage 4 and above.

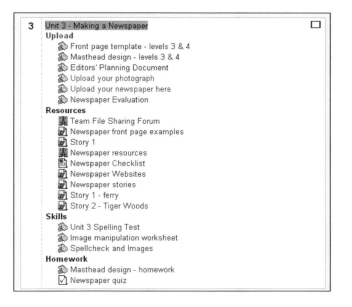

Figure 6.1 Example of possible folder structure

Assessment and testing

The VLE can be used to support 'assessment for learning' and 'assessment of learning'. Black and Wiliam (1998) put together over 240 research papers that support assessment for learning and found that regular assessment of learning is very motivating and helps to improve self-esteem and results. 'Assessment for learning' extends regular formative assessments to feedback and target setting. When pupils know and understand their targets, they are more motivated. Using the VLE, your pupils can upload their completed work, and you can mark it and return it to them along with feedback and targets for development. It would be sensible to go back to Chapter 3 to look at the assessment objects. You can also set different assessment grading types to reflect the requirements of the different key stages.

For summative marking the VLE can aid your role. Pupils can submit their work via the VLE, and you can assess it following the key stage criteria. Marks will automatically be transferred to the gradebook (see Chapter 3). These data can then be used to project estimated national test levels or grades. You can also use the VLE for setting end of year tests, or end of term tests, using a variety of question or assignment types to suit the learning needs of your groups. Results can often be output in the form of a spreadsheet or graph which can be used to report progress of whole groups, or for setting of groups the following year. Where you want students to work in groups for their projects, the VLE also supports group discussion, liaison, submission, and assessment.

Assessment of learning provides good opportunities to use praise more frequently, and to set achievable targets for your students to keep progressing. Some teachers are excellent at ensuring marks are recorded for every lesson, others less so. It is essential that you build a good monitoring record that records progress for each lesson for each group you teach. When you write your lesson plans, and decide on your learning objectives, you need to consider assessment for learning, i.e. how are you going to assess the learning of individual pupils. You can then use this information in planning your next lesson. If one objective is not achieved you may need to revisit it in the next lesson.

By ensuring that you apply assessment for learning to your planning cycle you start to build a picture of each individual pupil. When you look across your monitoring sheets, together with baseline data and predicted levels/grades, your picture becomes more complete and you can start to target those who are underachieving.

Reflective diaries

Many VLEs offer a learning object that enables pupils to keep a reflective diary. Students can add text to this over a period of time. They can set their own targets, which can be shared with you. This can be long-term evaluation of set targets, or it could be used in a lesson in which pupils have been asked to evaluate, for example, a newspaper article, or the front page of a comic/magazine, or a painting. These evaluations can then be shared with the rest of the group as a discussion; you could then set targets for development based on this. You could use this for a starter activity, in the plenary, or for homework. One successful way of using it is to ask students to evaluate their learning and progress in the lesson; this can be linked to your objectives, by identifying those they feel confident with and those that require more practice or support.

Peer review

Some VLEs have specific learning objects that allow the pupils to evaluate a set number of items of their peers' work. This is peer assessment and fits very nicely into the various National Strategies and the move to encourage pupils to feed back to each other and help set targets together in lessons. This can be done using pairs or small groups working collaboratively, who operate in the role of critical friend. When used in a supportive atmosphere, peer review can be used to extend each other's learning. There are social benefits to using this, but pupils will need coaching in developing these skills, and you may need to set ground rules to ensure the comments remain positive. You need to monitor their reactions carefully to ensure your pupils do not lose self-esteem. However, it is an excellent way of developing pupils' abilities to assess, provide feedback, and learn how to use criteria. Some GCSE modules allow peers to grade each other's work and this can be used for the final grading for that piece of work. Peer assessment skills can start to be developed at primary school, and extended to include national test or awarding body criteria with older classes.

In the same way pupils can be encouraged to assess their own work, using similar techniques, called self-assessment. You need to provide them with some criteria to use: this can be very simple for younger learners, moving to exam board criteria for older pupils. This helps to build pupils into better learners and develops a deeper insight into the assessment process. They may need to be trained so they understand the rationale, but practice will help them. Remember that when you use self-assessment against exam board criteria, or National Curriculum levels, you may need to put the language into pupil-friendly phrases.

Variety is one of the major advantages of a VLE. As stated in the previous section, it is very simple to create a whole range of different teaching strategies that cover all of the different learning styles in your classroom. The VLE is in itself a different teaching strategy that appeals to different learning styles. Go back to the reflective task in the previous section. Some examples of how a VLE can be used for learning styles are:

- **visual: mind maps, diagrams, animations, video clips, etc;**
- **auditory: MP3 files, narration, sound effects, news reports, podcasts, radio programme excerpts, etc;**
- **kinaesthetic: modelling of movements which pupils need to practise, learning to use a keyboard, step-by-step instructions for practical tasks, learning musical instruments, etc.**

Within the lesson structure the VLE can be used to provide variety at each stage of the lesson. For example, you can introduce the lesson with a starter activity accessed via the VLE, use it again for the main part of the lesson, and ask pupils to evaluate their progress via the VLE in the plenary. For assessment for learning, you can ask the pupils to upload their work so you can return it with feedback and targets, or have a quiz that tests their individual understanding of the topic. For younger pupils you can make the quiz more interactive and fun by using a familiar concept such as 'Hangman'. Examples can be found on the internet and there are some useful links at the end of this chapter. Go back to Chapter 3 to look at the wide variety of objects available.

E-portfolios and formative and summative assessment

E-portfolios are increasingly being used in schools (see Chapter 5). An e-portfolio is a collection of a pupil's work which enables formative and summative assessment. It can be a very small project, or can extend to a very large portfolio. It may be a simple collection of documents in a folder, or a more elaborate document using a website which the pupil has created. In secondary education there is an increasing requirement for e-portfolios by exam boards, e.g. the new DiDA suite of qualifications in ICT. As exam boards move more to electronic marking, it is likely this will expand.

At a very basic level you can start to use these in teaching with a project that the pupils need to do, and showing them how to save it using folders. They can then email you via the VLE when their project is ready for marking. You can then review it and provide feedback and targets for development via the VLE. Even the most basic VLEs have a facility for pupils to compress their website into a single file, then upload it for the teacher to review. Pupils at primary level, especially those with learning difficulties, might find this more challenging, but you could support it with a step-by-step wall display using graphic images for them to refer to.

The National Curriculum for ICT introduces pupils to web design in Years 5 and 6. As pupils become more confident users of ICT they will want to develop their own web pages. The development of an e-portfolio is a good vehicle for teaching these skills while the project develops. Again, these can be very basic for Key Stage 2 pupils, and develop in complexity as they learn new skills in their ICT lessons at later key stages. When using e-portfolios, web design and blogging with pupils you need to be aware of the safety issues for the pupils if they are going to be open to people outside the school. A range of organisations provide excellent information on managing this aspect of your teaching – see the web links at the end of this chapter. You also need to be aware of your school policy and guidelines on this issue.

Some VLEs have specific learning objects to create e-portfolios while others have the facility for pupils to create a website. For the more complex portfolios, pupils would create a series of web pages which explain the rationale behind their work and how they created it, and will provide a link to the work itself. For more help on how to design a website, or teach web design skills, go to Becta; or Amazon have a range of good web design books from primary level upwards.

At Key Stages 4 and 5 awarding body requirements vary. It is very important if you are preparing pupils for course work submission to read the awarding body specification carefully to ensure you are using the acceptable file format. It can be very time-consuming to convert a whole class of files for the exam board. Not all exam boards are yet able to accept e-portfolios, but this is an area they are all developing.

Some schools are now starting to use e-portfolios in their middle/primary sector, for the pupils to take with them to their next school. Many secondary schools are developing bridging units with their feeder schools that comprise an e-portfolio of achievements, or a specific project that can be further developed after transition. This is proving very successful. This serves several purposes. It:

- **demonstrates to their new teachers what level they are at in a variety of subjects;**
- **allows pupils to 'show off' their best work and helps to raise their confidence and self-esteem in their new school;**
- **helps to develop skills that will be used in later key stages.**

E-portfolios can also be used for pupils to build up evidence for their career, or university application. This can comprise achievements, extracurricular activities, grades, etc. It is expected that this will ultimately replace the Progress File and will link closely to the Professional Development Profile used in higher education. Some vocational qualifications already require evidence of work experience, and by using the VLE for this, it can be accessed from outside the school, so pupils can develop their e-portfolio while on placement.

Learning objects and assessments

With a VLE you can grade pupils' results (see Chapter 3 for details). VLEs allow you to set the grading levels to suit the needs of your group. For example:

- **awarding body grading levels or outcomes for GCSEs, GCEs, etc.;**
- **school criteria, such as 1–10;**
- **national test levels.**

You can define your own levels so you can have custom levels such as pass, merit and distinction; or comments such as good, very good, satisfactory and poor; or A–F. You can use different grading types for different learning objects, but it is important to be consistent so that the pupils understand what the gradings mean. Parents can also be given access to the gradings for their child so that they can monitor progress.

You may want to consider giving the pupils the 'value-added' grading; this can motivate them to achieve higher results. With this system, rather than giving them the grading level you give them a +1 or –1. For example, if a pupil is predicted to get a level 4 in a subject and they are working at level 5, they get a +1; alternatively, if they are predicted to get a grade D at GCSE and are working at a grade E, they get a –1.

The majority of assessed material is likely to take the form of assignments or quizzes. Details of how to use these can be found in Chapter 3.

If setting assignments for course work it is important that the work is split into logical sections so that it is easily understandable by the pupils, and also by you, for marking. It is good practice to set deadlines throughout the year rather than having all parts of the course work due at the end of the year, as this helps pupils with their time management. It also provides opportunities for feedback, target setting linked to awarding body criteria, and revisions. Throughout course work it is essential to make links to the mark scheme and also provide exemplar work to guide pupils.

To aid pupils in revision it is useful to provide examples of past exam papers, links to awarding body websites, specific exam questions, along with the mark scheme and examiners' comments. This may not all be of relevance to younger pupils.

It is important to set regular homework that serves a purpose. For example, it might be to consolidate some learning that links to your lesson objectives, be evaluative or linked to target setting, or be a preparation for work to come. The homework can be set using the VLE for pupils and parents to access from home. Where not all of your pupils have access from home you need to remember to ensure that a paper version is available. Pupils do appear to be more motivated to complete homework that is set via a VLE. When it is complete the pupils upload this for you to mark, making the process more rapid as there is no need to wait for the next lesson to collect it, thereby enabling it to be used in your planning for your next lesson. Settings within the VLE allow you to be automatically notified when work has been submitted, and for the pupil to be notified automatically when it has been returned with feedback and, where appropriate, targets. The Standards site has more help and information on setting homework – see the end of this chapter for the link.

Most VLEs allow the setting of deadlines for quizzes, assignments, homework, etc. Most also link this automatically to the calendar facility which will, in turn, highlight the deadlines for them. Many systems can be set to give reminders of deadlines in advance.

It is important, where possible, to involve parents/carers in the progress of their children. This is going to become increasingly important as the *Every Child Matters* agenda develops. Some parents may never be interested, but the vast majority are interested and want to support their children's development. Many VLE systems allow parents to access the calendar to see when work is due in, what marks/grades are given, the feedback, targets, and homework deadlines, etc. By using this facility they can have a shared role with you to increase support and motivation. Some VLEs automatically generate passwords and usernames for parents to access their child's area. Facility is often made for parents to contact teachers to query issues. This could impact on your workload, but should be carefully managed by the school.

As with all assessments, when using the VLE to assess work, you need to consider the development of higher-order skills such as analysis, reasoning and evaluating. Pupils who are less able may need assessments that link to lower-order skills such as developing ideas, expressing opinions, and responses to triggers. Variety is an important aspect, so don't keep using one form of assessment. You need to write your assessments carefully to motivate your students to develop. The great power of the VLE is the wide range of the assessments you can use and the social interaction you can build into your assessments.

PRACTICAL TASK PRACTICAL TASK **PRACTICAL** TASK PRACTICAL TASK **PRACTICAL** TASK

Using an assignment you have used with a group recently, break this into higher-order and lower-order skills. Now write these as a VLE assessment and trial them with a different group. Evaluate the differences. Remember to indicate which level the assessment is aimed at, to develop independent learning.

Feedback and target setting

Feedback and target setting are very important to the progress of your pupils and provide the scaffold between their actual performance and the desired level of their performance. This may be based on in-school data, or value-added data. By receiving positive feedback with achievable and realistic targets, not only can you motivate your pupils to achieve more, and stimulate the correction of errors, but you can also encourage them to develop independent learning skills. When giving any feedback you need to focus on the knowledge and skills/concepts you need them to know and understand. It needs to be detailed and constructive, and you need to provide it promptly, so that it is meaningful to them. It is also important that you personalise their feedback, setting individual targets for development. Ideally your feedback should be task-focused and start by acknowledging their strengths, before moving to the areas that you want them to target and develop further. Aim to challenge your students and provide feedback which engages and stimulates them to improve their performance – see Figure 6.2.

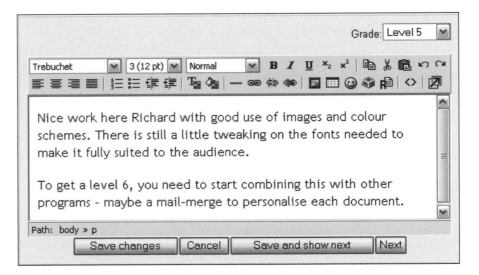

Figure 6.2 Example of constructive feedback and target setting

By using the VLE for pupils to upload their work for you to assess, you can provide both feedback and targets that can then be shared with them, accessed by parents, and recorded for you to assess overall progress towards grades/levels. With many VLEs you can set up a system that informs you as soon as work has been submitted. A record will be kept on the VLE of the whole group, indicating who has submitted, who submitted work late, whose work you have marked, and whose work you still need to mark. Systems may exist to apply penalties for late work.

When you open up their work you will be able to add comments, either in the feedback area, or some VLEs let you add comments into their work, in the same way that you would annotate work if you were assessing it by hand. Be aware that although Word has a comment system, some VLEs won't allow you to save the comments back into the pupils' work on the VLE; you therefore need to ensure you use the system within the VLE.

Some VLEs also have a separate 'Target' section which allows all teachers of that pupil to monitor targets, which can be very useful. Remember that when you are setting targets they need to be SMART: specific, measurable, achievable, realistic and time-related (Brooks, 2002). Some systems also allow pupils to comment on progress towards targets, can be used in the plenary section of your lesson, and encourage the pupils to evaluate their own progress towards these targets. Many VLEs allow parents to be involved in setting and monitoring targets to give additional support.

When you have finished assessing the work, you need to save the feedback. Depending on the VLE you are using, the pupil then receives a message that their work has been assessed and commented on. With some VLEs you can set up a further system of alerting to let you know they have received their work.

When giving feedback it is important to be positive. If they are working towards specific exam board criteria you need to give the feedback in terms of these criteria so they can see where they are losing marks or could easily gain additional marks. You can also point them to additional work to support their learning. For example, if your pupils were a Key Stage 2 mathematics group and they had not understood a concept, you can refer them to additional tasks on your VLE that revise the concept, or link them to a website to support this aspect of their learning.

Once work has been uploaded it can be used to standardise and level work between different teachers. It could also be done across different schools if they had compatible VLEs. It would be simple to discuss the levels by using the forum facility. LEA advisors could also be involved with this process to give advice if needed. This process can be used for internal moderation. You may want to share the grades of the whole group, which you can do via the VLE. This can often help pupils to focus on their own grades, and motivate them to improve against their peers' grades.

As a trainee or NQT your marking could be monitored closely by your mentor, particularly where it is a new topic or qualification for you. Your feedback and targets could also be monitored to provide you with additional support. Once you have qualified, your head of department or co-ordinator could use the VLE to monitor your marking in terms of timeliness, accuracy and feedback to continue to help you develop.

Using your scheme of work, identify a lesson you are going to teach in the next few weeks that is mainly assessed using questions. Look at how it is currently assessed and how you can break this down for uploading to the VLE. Match this with the different types of questions available in your VLE. You also need to consider the grading method you are going to use. Create a quiz and some questions to support this. Upload it to your VLE and pilot it with a group of pupils. What changes, if any, do you need to make?

Using a VLE for assessment

This is an example of how one school in the East Midlands used a VLE to develop the focus of assessment. The school was 11–18, but the focus could easily be transferred to primary teaching.

Assessment was being used traditionally and feedback was provided formatively and summatively by most staff. However, it was felt by senior management that this was an area that needed further development and it was agreed to use the VLE as a vehicle for improvement. Initially one exam course was chosen as a pilot.

For the chosen course the teachers involved divided the course into manageable areas, having decided on where and when assessment would take place. Each piece of work that was to be assessed was linked to the exam board criteria and mark schemes. A variety of assessment methods were identified, taking into account the inclusive elements of assessment such as writing frames for the less able, and methods of assessing the small percentage of EAL pupils. By identifying a range of methods, the teachers were also able to ensure that all learning styles were provided with an opportunity to succeed. In addition, the teachers were able to ensure that the more able were adequately challenged through extension work and a range of higher-level tasks.

The organisation within the VLE was clear, showing assessment linked to resources for the topic. Pupils were guided to the relevant assessments and levels.

When pupils had completed their assessments they submitted them automatically to their teachers, who in turn received notification of the submission. Teachers were able to mark the assessments using in-line commenting, and return the work together with individual targets and feedback.

When the assessment was completed, the grade/mark was then recorded within the VLE. This allowed the pupil to monitor their own progress against their targets. It also enabled the teachers to monitor progress and link this to targets, and value-added targets.

Many of the research findings for Chapter 3 are also applicable to this chapter. In addition, Ulicsak (2004) found that pupils exhibited improved retention when using computer-mediated self-assessment, and they spent more time reflecting on group behaviour when they thought they were being observed by the system. Doherty (1998) and Chou and Liu (2005) stress the importance of learner control in an online learning experience. This can be reflected in your choice of tasks and mode of assessment. In 2003 Becta produced a meta-study of the research concerning VLEs in secondary schools, how effective they were, and the implications for teachers and managers.

CHAPTER **SUMMARY**

This chapter has helped you to start to use a range of tests, tasks and assessments on your VLE.

Try to address a range of learning styles when creating your tasks, tests and assessments for your VLE.

Ensure that your pupils have the necessary support materials when accessing your VLE from home.

Make good use of the calendar facility to encourage your pupils to submit work on time, and plan their own time management.

Develop your skills in providing feedback and target setting via the VLE.

Consider ways of building in multimedia to address inclusion issues.

What next?

Using the VLE, you are now able to implement tasks, tests and assessment into your own teaching. Start by experimenting with the different facilities we have discussed in this chapter, and try them out with your pupils. You will find different groups react differently to the range of tests and tasks available to you to use with the VLE. Remember to reflect on the good practice we have discussed in this chapter, and consider asking some of your peers to look at the feedback and targets you are giving to your pupils. This will help you to develop professionally so that you know you are giving detailed and comprehensive feedback to all your pupils.

Useful websites

http://audacity.sourceforge.net/ – link to download Audacity software, an excellent, and free, package for recording. This is the software recommended for schools by the DfES. The site also provides support for using the software.

www.acceleratedlearning.com – good discussion of education and Gardner's multiple intelligences. Includes an online multiple intelligence inventory.

www.britishcouncil.org – a useful resource to refer to when teaching pupils with EAL. Also useful for establishing links with schools abroad.

www.englishlearners.com/hangman/index.html and **www.planetquiz.com** – have examples of hangman-based quizzes for different subjects.

www.everychildmatters.gov.uk – provides information on this agenda, together with a range of resources and information.

www.jisc.ac.uk – the Joint Information Systems Committee, a site aimed at supporting the use of ICT in further and higher education. It has a great deal of useful information and research about the use of learning objects in different scenarios.

www.moodle.org – the official site for the open-source VLE, Moodle. Through the forums, it offers a wide variety of discussions about issues faced when designing tasks and assessments, and when feeding back.

www.notschool.net – this site has been designed to support children who do not attend school for a variety of reasons.

www.safekids.com/ and **www.becta.org.uk** – provide good information for using the internet safely. Becta provide an excellent pack, which you can order free from their website.

www.standards.dfes.gov.uk/ – provides help and information on setting appropriate homework. There are also some useful case studies.

www.standards.dfes.gov.uk/keystage3/ – provides useful documents, which support teaching EAL students within the curriculum.

www.teachernet.gov.uk – this has a range of information on learning styles, together with links to related websites. By doing a search on 'learning styles' you will find a range of useful links including the visual, auditory and kinaesthetic styles referred to in this chapter.

REFERENCES REFERENCES **REFERENCES** REFERENCES **REFERENCES** REFERENCES

Becta (2003) *A review of the research literature on the use of managed learning environments and virtual learning environments in education, and a consideration of the implications for schools in the United Kingdom*. Coventry: BECTa.

Chou, S W and Liu, C H (2005) Learning effectiveness in a web-based virtual learning environment: a learner control perspective, *Journal of Computer Assisted Learning*, 21, 65–76.

Doherty, P (1998) Learner control in asynchronous learning environments, *Asynchronous Learning Networks Magazine,* 2, 2.

Ulicsak, M (2004) 'How did it know we weren't talking?': An investigation into the impact of self-assessments and feedback in a group activity, *Journal of Computer Assisted Learning*, 20, 205–211.

FURTHER READING   FURTHER READING   **FURTHER READING**   FURTHER READING

Black, P and Wiliam, D (1998) *Inside the black box.* London: King's College.

Brooks, V (2002) *Assessment in secondary schools.* Buckingham: Open University Press.

Wood, D (1998) *How children think and learn*. Oxford: Blackwell.

Wragg, E C (2001) *Assessment and children's learning in the primary school (successful teaching).* Abingdon: RoutledgeFalmer.

7
Design issues –
how to design virtual learning

By the end of this chapter you should be able to:

- design content which meets the needs of your learners;
- understand how text and images can be used to give an appropriate look and feel to content;
- organise content into lessons and series of lessons;
- make choices about using different media.

This chapter addresses the following Professional Standards for QTS:

Q8, Q10, Q17, Q18, Q19, Q23, Q24, Q25, Q29

Introduction

As VLEs become more and more sophisticated, it is increasingly easy to alter the 'look and feel' of learning environment. Issues of organising content, designing materials to be read on screen, and presenting ideas through other media are examined. The design of your virtual learning environment is as important to teaching and learning as a real learning environment. In designing your VLE you will need to take into account a number of issues, including:

- colours;
- logos;
- layout;
- text size and style;
- images.

Design issues

Designing a virtual learning environment is as complex as designing a real classroom and school. You need to take several factors into consideration, including:

- the ways you will teach;
- the ways the pupils will learn;
- other people who may use the space (parents, teaching assistants, other members of the school community);
- the types of learning you want to encourage;
- the types of resources you want to use;
- the ways that the users of the space will communicate;
- how you want the space to look and feel in response to all of all of the above.

Before you start work on designing your VLE, you need to think about the answers to these questions. Problems with VLEs occur when they are created without planning, the result often ending up complex or disorganised as it develops in response to the needs of the teachers and learners. The best way to approach a VLE is to work in systematic stages. The following process will be helpful in doing this.

Step 1 look and feel

VLEs allow you to change the way your pages will appear. Choosing the right layout, colours and texts is very important. Generally speaking it is best to keep things clear and plain. The choice of colour could reflect the class name, or the school's colours or the National Curriculum subject. It is inadvisable to use too many decorations or pictures. However, it is a good idea to title and 'brand' the VLE clearly with the school, class or subject, and many VLEs will allow you to add the school's logo to the homepage. This helps to build the right look and feel for a learning environment. It is important to remember that learners pick up clues about how to behave in a learning environment (real or virtual) from everything there – it is not just about the text and the content.

Step 2 tools and communication

VLEs have a wide range of tools or learning objects available for use. It is highly unlikely that you will use them all in one VLE or one project. Chapter 3 discusses these individually, but as a guide you are likely to be able to add some or all of the following:

- calendar;
- events/news/notices;
- tasks box;
- assignments;
- quizzes;
- choice/voting tool;
- email;
- discussion board;
- chat/instant messaging;
- electronic portfolios;
- content (text and images);
- movies;
- links to websites;
- filing areas.

In designing the VLE for a specific task, you should consider which of these (as a guide, no more than five for primary phase and eight for secondary phase) you are going to use. It is easier to add tools and content when you need them than have empty/unused links on your page. This makes the homepage clear and helps to keep learners focused on the most relevant tasks.

Step 3 reviewing your design

As your use of the VLE develops with pupils, you will probably extend and expand the range of tools, content and communication you use. It is much better to start small and manageable and develop the range of tools and uses as pupils and other users get more confident and adept at using the VLE. The following are some examples of ways you could design a basic VLE, and ways you could adapt and improve your design as the students and other users become used to the VLE. These principles should be used when reviewing your design.

- **Keep the number of tools minimal and under review.**
- **Choose colours which will help students to find their way around.**
- **Use pictures/icons where possible.**
- **Keep the number of clicks down to a minimum.**
- **Add new tools gradually.**

Typical uses

Primary:

You can alter the look and feel of your VLE using different colours and designs. Some may be suitable for younger pupils. Younger pupils or those who find text difficult (for instance, those with a learning disability or a visual impairment) will find it easier to work with clear icons like the ones in Figure 7.1, along with coloured areas. It's also important to try to prevent 'web drift' by limiting the number of clicks pupils need to make to locate a resource. Figure 7.1 uses large icons and colours that support pupils' navigation and has only three tools, a noticeboard, a text and image file, and a class calendar. Where other tools need to be added, such as electronic portfolios, it is advisable to do this one tool at a time. The maximum number of tools should probably be fewer than five to help pupils stay focused on tasks in hand.

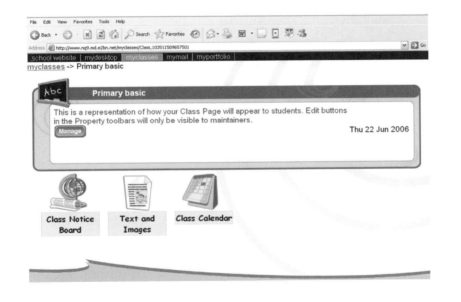

Figure 7.1 Example of a basic VLE design for the primary phase

Secondary:

Design for older or more able pupils is not necessarily more complex. The same rules apply as for primary:

- Keep the number of tools minimal and under review.
- Choose colours which will help students to find their way around.

- Use pictures/icons where possible.
- Keep the number of clicks down to a minimum.
- Add new tools gradually.

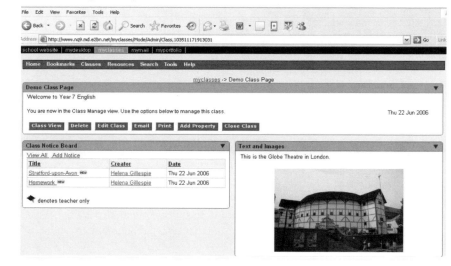

Figure 7.2 Example of a basic VLE design for the secondary phase

Figure 7.2 shows a design that could be used as a starting point for designing a VLE for secondary phase pupils. It contains a section for notices and some text and images related to ongoing work. Tools can be introduced gradually to pupils, but the overall number can be more than the five recommended with primary phase pupils, depending on how able the students are and what use the tools are being put to.

A design for a secondary phase VLE might differ from a primary phase one in the following ways:

- **more links to the internet;**
- **wider choice of tools and materials;**
- **more text;**
- **wider range of images;**
- **more 'levels' or clicks in the design so more materials can be stored.**

PRACTICAL TASK PRACTICAL TASK PRACTICAL TASK PRACTICAL TASK PRACTICAL TASK

Plan a well-designed VLE.

- **For the group or groups you are working with, begin to design a VLE by making a list of what you want to use it for in the short, medium and long term.**

- **Examine the various 'look and feel' options offered by your VLE and choose the one that seems best suited to your needs.**

- **Consult colleagues about VLEs they have used and designed – what has worked for them?**

- **Once you have made your VLE, watch pupils using it. Do they find the navigation easy?**

- **Ask pupils what they think of the design and how they would like it to be improved.**

Using text and images – choosing the right media

Most teachers are now used to producing teaching and learning materials in electronic form. These might include:

- **worksheets and information sheets;**
- **charts and graphs containing data;**
- **still and moving images;**
- **multimedia presentations.**

There is a wealth of media available to teachers now in electronic form on the internet. These include:

- **texts, literature and written sources of evidence;**
- **online games and activities;**
- **still and moving images;**
- **diaries and blogs.**

The range and scope of materials available continues to expand and Becta are developing a programme which should help assess the quality and usefulness of different tools in different contexts (Becta, 2005a).

Given this range of resources that could be made accessible using a VLE, you must think carefully which ones you want to use. Consider the resources as you would in your face-to-face teaching, thinking about how, when and why you want pupils to use them. On a VLE you can upload content you have made yourself (see list above) for pupils to use. This can be supplemented by links to online content. How these elements can be used and developed is discussed in the section below on organising content into lessons.

Typical uses

Primary:

These are examples of activities that could be delivered by a VLE. They need to be carefully planned for and used in teaching. The next section deals in more detail with how to include virtual learning in face-to-face lessons, as does Chapter 2 on blended learning.

English – provide a piece of text for pupils to work on. It might be the beginning of a story, or a piece that needs correcting or the work of another pupil for collaborative writing.

Mathematics – simple spreadsheets make investigating patterns in numbers easy. Provide pupils with a spreadsheet to investigate repeated addition, or work out tables.

Science – pictures are important in developing pupils' understanding of scientific ideas and concepts. Providing electronic pictures allows pupils not only to look at images but also to use them in their own work and save them. These might be images taken with a digital camera by the teacher or by pupils.

History – using primary evidence in history makes lessons more exciting for pupils and can help them develop the skills of historical enquiry that they need for later study. Video and audio files of people talking about their histories – these might be children, parents or grandparents –

---

can be provided for pupils to listen to, watch and use in their own work and at their own pace.

When providing these sorts of electronic resources for primary school pupils, you need to consider how to make these accessible in simple ways. It is worth checking which file formats are best to use, and in the case of audio and video files, which format these will play in. It might be that pupils need to be paired or to work with an adult to develop the appropriate ICT skills they need to be able to use the resources effectively.

Secondary:
These are examples of activities that could be delivered by a VLE. They need to be carefully planned for and used in teaching. The next section deals in more detail with how to include virtual learning in face-to-face lessons, as does Chapter 2 on blended learning.

English – Wikipedia, the online editable encyclopaedia (http://en.wikipedia.org), has become a very popular website over the past few years, and as a result web-based 'wiki' tools have begun to appear. In essence these are web pages that are editable by a group of people, enabling them to come to a shared description or definition. These could be useful in defining genres, types of literature or individual words in the study of texts. Free wikis are available at http://pbwiki.com/edu.html and many VLEs now have an add-in wiki tool. This kind of instant publishing is good for encouraging pupils to think about the style of their writing and to consider the audience.

Mathematics – spreadsheets can be designed for a number of purposes, and getting pupils to design their own is a useful and creative activity. For example, creating a spreadsheet that is able to calculate a league table, and then sharing this, would enable pupils to see the outcome of various football results.

Science – electronic microscopes that can be connected to computers produce high-quality images of cells and other very small things for study. Pupils can create and share these images that are useful for course work.

History – blogging is another recent development in web-based technology and enables users to record their ideas in the form of a web log (blog). These can also be used by a group of contributors or an individual to record ideas – this might be a place where pupils can discuss and develop their historical research.

REFLECTIVE TASK

Consider the range of tasks you want to do in a unit of work or week. Ask yourself these questions:

- **Which tasks do you want pupils to undertake?**
- **In what order?**
- **Can you hide or remove any tools or resources to make things simpler?**

Organising content into lessons – teaching and learning tips

Personalised learning

The design of a VLE should be influenced by the needs of those who use it. This will include teachers and pupils, but may also include other school staff such as teaching assistants, school managers and also parents and carers of pupils. Clearly these needs will be different for groups of pupils or even for individual pupils. At first this may seem like an impossible task – to design a VLE for each pupil – but used thoughtfully, a VLE could help meet the needs of individuals. In the Futurelab report on personalised learning (Green, Facer et al, 2005) and the Learner Charter for a personalised learning environment, the authors make the case for adapting teaching methods which can meet the needs of diverse learners and in some cases even make provision for the offer of 'bespoke support' to learners. In designing your VLE for your lessons, you should consider how the available tools could help meet the needs of individual pupils.

Blending learning

Chapter 2 covers blended learning in detail. However, it is useful to mention some of the main points when considering VLE design issues, as the VLE design will need to be considered when planning the lesson or lessons in which the VLE will be used.

The structure of the lesson

In both primary and secondary schools, the three-part lesson is commonplace. A VLE can fit well into any of these elements. For example, some aspects can be used as part of an introductory demonstration, or pupils can use resources and activities set up in the main part of the lesson, or share their work as part of a plenary. However, a well-designed VLE can also help teachers develop a range of lessons that might not fit this structure. A teacher could ask pupils to use a blog to collect ideas before starting a new topic, or let pupils explore a range of internet links before introducing the topic in the face-to-face part of the lesson. Most importantly, teachers need to consider how best to plan for the use of the VLE within schemes and established plans of lessons.

Timing

When you first start out as a teacher on professional placement in schools, one of the most difficult aspects of classroom management to master is lesson timing. Using technology in lessons can only make this more difficult. However, if you consider the following you should be able to plan carefully for the time it takes to use technology and get the lesson timing to work.

- How long does it take to get out/switch on/log on?
- How fast is the connection to the network?
- How well practised are the pupils in using the skills needed (see below)?

Group and individual work

Effective collaborative work among pupils is challenging to achieve in any phase. It takes careful planning on the part of the teacher and impacts on time, resources and teaching approaches. This is even trickier when you are trying to include the use of technology in a lesson. It's important when you are planning for pupils to collaborate that you define roles clearly; for instance, one pupil might take on part of the research, the other may lead on putting together a presentation to be uploaded. In addition, many collaborative VLE lessons would involve the use of email or discussion boards. It's important to make it clear to pupils when, how and in what ways you expect them to communicate.

Pupils' skills

Pupils in the same class may have varied attitudes to and aptitudes for using virtual learning tools. These differences need to be taken into account in planning, allowing for extra adult or peer support where necessary and having additional tasks to hand if necessary. To be able to plan for all of this effectively it's important to understand the pupils' skills and attitudes. Assessing and tracking the development of skills in using virtual learning tools is useful in this way.

Learning out of school

Many schools in the secondary phase are now using virtual learning environments to support the development of homework and other out-of-school work such as course work. There are also useful applications in the primary phase in getting pupils and their families involved in learning together. These opportunities can be planned into schemes of lessons.

VLEs and ICT tools

There is a wide range of ICT tools in schools now, which teachers can use in creative and engaging teaching. They can be used in conjunction with a VLE in a variety of ways:

- *Digital camera* – a digital camera is a versatile tool not only because it enables pupils to express ideas in images, but also because those images can instantly be shared via a VLE.
- *Interactive whiteboard* – increasingly classrooms are equipped with IWBs which enable teachers to interact with technology in ways the whole class can see and join in with. An IWB can be used to demonstrate and share resources on the IWB with the whole class. In addition, it enables teachers to use the VLE to store teaching materials and resources to be shared with pupils in direct face-to-face teaching and then make them available online via the VLE.
- *Handheld computers (PDAs)* – handheld computers are increasingly used in situations where pupils need to be mobile, on the sports field, in a drama lesson or in the science lab. Handheld computers connected to a wireless network mean that the users can connect to the internet at any time. They enable pupils to use resources and communication tools on the VLE in a wider variety of learning situations.

PRACTICAL TASK PRACTICAL TASK **PRACTICAL TASK** PRACTICAL TASK **PRACTICAL TASK**

Consider the elements above and ask these questions when planning lessons and series of lessons:

- In which part of the lesson would virtual learning fit best?
- How long will it take? Is this a good use of learning time?
- Do I want pupils to work individually or in groups? How should I organise the technology to make this happen?
- What skills do my pupils have? Are these sufficient to undertake the tasks they are being asked to do?
- Can the VLE support learning in this topic/subject outside the classroom?

RESEARCH SUMMARY RESEARCH SUMMARY RESEARCH SUMMARY RESEARCH SUMMARY

The Futurelab report on personalised learning is thought-provoking and challenging. In addition, the Learner Charter for a personalised learning environment published alongside this is an important starting point for those who want to learn more about how virtual learning can be used to contribute to an offer of more personalised learning to pupils. It can be downloaded from the Futurelab website, *www.futurelab.org.uk/research/personalisation/report_01.htm*. As the development of learning platforms and virtual learning environments progresses, Becta will continue to give advice on this important aspect of ICT development (Becta, 2005b).

CHAPTER **SUMMARY**

This chapter is about design issues. It consolidates and builds on advice given in other chapters about the teaching and learning materials that can be used in virtual learning, and how they are best organised.

Advice about planning lessons that include a virtual learning element is given, as well as some ideas about how individual tools might be used. Issues such as differentiation and personalisation have been raised.

There are some suggestions for using a variety of ICT devices in conjunction with a VLE.

What next?

Consider how the design and delivery of virtual learning can support your pupils and help you teach in ways that meet their needs. Keep an eye out for information about personalised learning – this will be a big issue over the next few years.

FURTHER READING FURTHER READING **FURTHER** READING FURTHER READING

Becta (2005a) *BECTa's view. A quality framework for e-learning resources*. Coventry: Becta.

Becta (2005b) *An introduction to learning platforms*. Coventry: Becta.

Green, H, Facer, K et al (2005) *Report on personalisation and digital technologies*. Bristol: Futurelab.

8
Introducing a VLE into school

By the end of this chapter you should be able to:
- **identify the technical and resourcing requirements on a macro and meso level needed for the introduction of a VLE;**
- **develop strategies to raise staff enthusiasm and participation in using the VLE, and organise training;**
- **plan for the introduction of a VLE and develop skills to be able to upload a range of resources.**

This chapter addresses the following Professional Standards for QTS:
Q4, Q5, Q6, Q7, Q8, Q12, Q14, Q19, Q22, Q24, Q29, Q30, Q32, Q33

Introduction

This chapter has been included to help you to set up a VLE, either for the use of the whole school when you start your full-time teaching post, or for use by yourself in your own teaching while on teaching practice. The advantage of the latter is that as you move to different placement schools you can develop your resources to meet your different teaching needs.

We have included general advice from an experienced team of teachers who have used VLEs to enhance their teaching and learning. This identifies how to download and set up a free VLE available from the internet that will run on most networks or personal computers/laptops, or use a purchased VLE. It also provides advice on how to involve a range of other staff, including teaching assistants and support staff, in developing the VLE. This could be relevant to you either in the capacity of a teacher introducing a VLE into the school as a way of enhancing your professional role, or as part of a wider team looking at introducing a VLE into the whole school. The majority of the sections described here are relevant to both scenarios.

As with all ICT-based projects of a substantial nature, the introduction of a VLE into a school needs to be carried out in a planned way. This is usually done as part of the 'systems life cycle'. The main stages of this are as follows.

Identify your needs

The initial 'problem' or need is the stimulus for the introduction of a VLE. At the whole-school level this could vary, but may include factors such as the enthusiasm of a group of staff who want to introduce blended learning, and believe the VLE is the best way to do this; national test levels not reaching those predicted; a need to increase GCSE results; boys' under-achievement; a need to address students who cannot attend school for whatever reason; the need to address distance learning; etc. At this stage in your training, which will be more at an individual level, it may be because you want to use blended learning as a way of meeting different learning styles and increasing the motivation of your pupils. It may be that you have been introduced to VLEs through your teacher training and are keen to put into practice blended learning starting from small beginnings.

If you are asked to be part of a team introducing the VLE, or decide this is a project you would like to take on, you will need to carry out a feasibility study.

Feasibility study

Several aspects need to be considered in deciding if a VLE is an appropriate solution, and if so, which VLE. At this stage, there is limited information about the VLE to be used, and the conditions it will be used in, so any decisions made at this stage must be general in nature.

Technical feasibility

Any VLE needs a commitment in terms of infrastructure. This can be separated into hardware and software, and whether it is to be introduced into the whole school or for your personal use while doing your teacher training.

Hardware

A web server is normally required, as the majority of VLEs are delivered via a web browser. For the whole-school installation this is also likely to be accessible from outside the school so that students and staff can access it from home. The web server could be located in a variety of places.

- **It may be within the school, with the school or third party managing and maintaining the server. This allows maximum control over the VLE, fast access, and a minimum cost, but requires a suitable level of technical support.**
- **It could be held by a third party such as a web-hosting company. This means that the management of the hardware, and possibly the operating system, are the responsibility of someone else. However, it is important to choose a host carefully, as not all hosting services are compatible with all VLEs. The hosting company also manages aspects such as firewalls and virus protection. Research on hosting companies will show which ones have the highest percentage 'uptime' and highest data transfer speeds. This could be particularly important if you are planning to use video as part of your VLE. The school would have to manage the technical aspects of the VLE itself remotely, which is not usually a problem.**
- **The company that provides the VLE may hold it. Solutions such as this are usually purchased as a whole from the VLE supplier. The school has minimal technical responsibilities and the vendor should be in a position of expertise to remedy problems as they arise. This is likely to be the most costly option.**

Bandwidth is also an important issue. In theory it is not necessary to have a broadband link to access a VLE but it is important to think about the file sizes which might be used and the downloading time required.

Specification – If you are installing the VLE for your personal use, most modern computers are sufficient to run it, but you will need internet and network connectivity to allow pupils access. Alternatively, hosting may be provided free of charge by your internet provider, or you can purchase space cheaply from a variety of sources located by doing a search on the

internet. You would normally maintain and manage your VLE yourself, although there may
be technical support within your placement school.

Software

Decide if the VLE requires software which you don't already have, such as a database. In
many cases, VLEs require open-source software, which is free.

Economic feasibility

The economic considerations can be split into two categories: the one-off capital costs of
setting up the VLE, and the ongoing costs.

If you are going to set up a small VLE for use on your teaching placements, or to 'try it out' in
a full-time teaching post, you will need a fairly up-to-date computer that has internet access
and some server space, which may be free with your internet provider. You will also need a
VLE package; some packages are available to trainee teachers via their teacher training
provider. Another option could be an open-source VLE, such as Moodle, which is free to
download. Instructions about how to download this are included at the end of this chapter.
Open-source software is free to download and can be customised to meet the needs of the
teacher and students; however, some technical expertise is needed in order to do this.
These 'free at the point of download' solutions such as Moodle will not in any way
reduce the objects you can use, or your pupils' access, which will be via the website URL
that you set up on the web server. Your pupils are then able to access it from anywhere in
the world once you have given them permission and a password. Parents are able to access
it in the same way. There are pros and cons associated with this approach, which are
discussed in more detail in Coppola and Neelley (2004).

If you want to use it on the school network the capital costs need to include the purchase of
the VLE, the initial costs of the web server, any costs involved with cabling and connectivity
and initial staff training.

Advantages of using an open-source VLE
- **Free to download;**
- **Full functionality;**
- **Well used and popular in schools;**
- **Customisable.**

Disadvantages of using an open-source VLE
- **Needs technical expertise to set up properly;**
- **Costs to maintain and train users;**
- **Technical support is not guaranteed.**

The ongoing costs of a VLE involve any yearly licences or subscriptions to the VLE, costs of
ongoing staff training, technical support, purchasing updates, paying for connectivity, and
renting a server if there is not one located within the school. It is important to be realistic
about these costs, otherwise an initial good idea could rapidly turn into something too costly
to run in the medium to long term.

Social feasibility

When considering the feasibility of installing your VLE it is important to take into account
whether all pupils have access to the VLE out of school via the internet. If they do not, or if

some of your pupils do not have internet access at home, you need to consider what steps can be taken to address this. You might decide that the benefits of the VLE in your teaching far outweighs this limitation, and plan to make any resources available on the VLE that pupils might want to access outside school time, available via hard copy.

If you are going to develop the VLE across a school, or team of enthusiasts, you need to consider whether staff are technically capable of acquiring the skills needed to successfully use the VLE, particularly in terms of creating and uploading the materials. Do you feel confident enough to run some staff training sessions? Your LEA may be able to help with staff training, or you may be able to join with other schools who are installing similar VLEs. Most VLEs also have a good help site, and often chat forums, so that you can ask for help and support virtually if you need it.

Legal feasibility

A VLE usually needs to keep personal details about its users, and as such is subject to the provisions of the Data Protection Act. Your school is probably already registered with the Data Protection Registrar, and so an onsite VLE should be covered. However, the situation should always be checked with the Registrar, particularly in cases where the VLE is hosted by another company. Obviously, the school needs to abide by the regulation in the Data Protection Act.

Although copyright should not be an issue, you and other staff need to be aware that software cannot be indiscriminately distributed via a VLE, and that electronic extracts are still covered by copyright legislation.

Some means must be provided for monitoring the use of the VLE, particularly the use of chat facilities and forums, to ensure that exchanges are not occurring which could be construed as bullying or intimidation. Failure to do so would leave the school open to litigation. Most VLEs allow you to give 'admin' rights to staff to help to monitor its use.

Timescale feasibility

If you are setting up your own VLE you might decide to start with one small course or project, evaluate its success and effectiveness, then expand it. You may decide to set up a larger course initially, particularly if you have most of your materials in electronic format already. If you are involved in a larger project that is cross-school, you need to consider how long the VLE will take to introduce and when it will be introduced. In some cases, too long a period of time will reduce the effectiveness of the VLE in terms of the initially identified need.

Scalability

It is important that any future growth of the VLE is taken into account. This may be due to unforeseen take-up of distance learning courses, linking of primary schools into the VLE of a secondary school, merging of schools, unforeseen school expansion, etc. This impacts on the choice of VLE and server specifications.

REFLECTIVE TASK

REFLECTIVE TASK

Taking all of these aspects into account, reflect on the main issues that will affect your VLE. Reflect on how you will address each one. For example, what aspects from the above do you need to address? Do you have the necessary hardware and software? Is there going to be a support system other than yourself? What is your timescale going to be – don't be over-ambitious and create stress for yourself. Also consider the materials you want to use – are any copyright-protected documents? How are you going to involve your students in the social aspects and encourage the different learning styles to make use of your VLEs?

Information to be gathered

During this stage of the life cycle, the information is gathered which influences many of the decisions about the future of the VLE. Without relevant information being gathered, it is likely that the decision made may not reflect the needs which are to be met. The information to be gathered includes the following.

Staff confidence with using ICT

By working through this book you will have gained in confidence and now be ready to use a VLE. In a situation where more staff are to be involved, the team will need to consider how confident the various users are with ICT. The more confident they are, the more likely they are to be receptive to the idea of using a VLE in their everyday teaching. They will also be easier to train and more likely to innovate.

It would be useful to map staff confidence and ability with ICT against departments, as this may affect the pattern of implementation later. Useful questionnaires for this can be found on the Becta website – refer to the list of websites at the end of this chapter.

Levels of student proficiency with ICT

The level to which students are able to use ICT may well affect the choice of VLE, as different VLEs have different characteristics with regard to ease of use. It may also affect the type of activities and learning objects which are used.

Technical support capacity

The number of ICT support staff and their technical ability could determine whether the school opts for a system operated entirely by the school, hosted elsewhere, or entirely operated by a third party. It may be that if current levels of support would not be adequate, further support could be bought in as part of the ongoing costs. This could be either someone employed by the school, or an outside party who could provide support via the internet. If you are working in a small primary school, with a lack of technical support, you may want to consider linking with your family secondary school if they have a VLE. With agreement, you should be able to develop an area on the VLE for yourself, or your school, to use and give permissions to your pupils. This may well develop into joint projects, which is very positive in the transfer of your pupils.

Technical aspects of the current system

The current computer system needs examining to ensure that it is compatible with a new VLE. The following aspects will need to be examined.

- Server specification – if a current server is to be used to host the VLE, it must be capable of continuing to provide its current service, alongside the new VLE. Aspects such as processor speed, disk space, memory, connectivity and bandwidth required all need to be considered.
- It is recommended that the situation is thoroughly discussed with the VLE provider. It must be borne in mind, however, that many providers may also sell their own servers, and so not be providing an unbiased opinion. Most VLE providers have a website where you can check the minimum specification they require.
- Network infrastructure – given that a VLE puts extra load on the current network, an analysis of current bandwidth used must be made to ensure that there is sufficient spare bandwidth to support a VLE. Also bear in mind that a VLE may well be delivering audio and video, which puts a much higher load on the network.
- Software – the new VLE may well require other specific software/operating systems which may not currently be present.

PRACTICAL TASK PRACTICAL TASK **PRACTICAL TASK** PRACTICAL TASK **PRACTICAL TASK**

Estimate the disk space required.

- Estimate the number of pieces of work/course work to be submitted per pupil.
- Assume a file size of 1MB for text files, 10MB for longer files with images, and 50MB for files of extended length with heavy image use. For a secondary school, multiply this by 10 to take into account other courses the pupil may be taking. For a primary school, you need to use your judgement depending on how the curriculum is delivered.
- Multiply this by the number of pupils in a year.
- Multiply this by the number of years in your school.
- Multiply this by 5 as an arbitrary life span in years of the VLE.
- Add 10 per cent to account for space used by quizzes, forums, etc.
- Add to this the space required for the operating system.

Teaching and learning styles

It is very important that you talk to the end users as part of the feasibility study. This includes the pupils and staff, and you may also want to involve some parents. Find out how they would like to use the VLE, when they might want to use it, and which of the objects (see Chapter 3), they would like to see implemented. What are the current difficulties they perceive in either teaching or learning – how can the VLE support this and help them to become more effective teachers and learners? You can find more information on this by referring to Chapter 2. You might want to consider a focus group for this, even if you are simply setting up a simple VLE for a small course/project. It is essential you consult with your end users.

Questions asked of staff could focus on finding out what their most pressing problems are, what factors are hindering them in their work. Which teaching and learning styles are most successful, and which new ones would they like to develop? It would be useful to find out what proportion of their teaching materials are in electronic format, and so would be simple to present on a VLE.

Prime questions for all groups would involve finding out what proportion have internet access at home, and the level of confidence of the users. An effective and efficient method of collecting this information could be to use a questionnaire. To make analysis of the results simpler, it would be useful to use a Likert scale for response. The scale is offered to indicate the degree of agreement with the answer, for example, 'How confident are you with using a computer – 1 = not at all ... 4 = very confident.' Further help with this can be found in Gillespie (2006).

Analysis

During this stage, the information which has been gathered is analysed with the objective of deciding which VLE to use, what hardware and software are required, and what the overall aims of the system are. These aims are used later to evaluate the system.

- **Software requirements – the decision about which VLE to use must be based on all the available information and be carried out in a way which involves representatives of all affected parties – teachers, pupils, managers, technical support, finance officer, etc. Failure to do so may leave groups of users feeling disenfranchised with no sense of ownership of the new VLE. It is also necessary to decide which operating system needs to be used, along with any other software that may be needed, such as plugins, etc. It may also be decided that the VLE has to communicate with the school's management information system (MIS).**
- **Hardware requirements – the minimum hardware requirements of the VLE must be taken as a starting point, bearing in mind that future possible expansion must be taken into account. This includes not only the server, but also the network infrastructure and internet connectivity.**
- **Requirements specification – this section must be carefully drawn up, as it affects all of the later stages, and what the VLE will eventually be able to do. The requirements specification should be a list of all the features of the VLE which are required. Implementation will not be considered successful unless all of the requirements have been met.**

Within this section do bear in mind that it is not all relevant if you are setting up a VLE for your own use with your pupils, rather than across the whole school, or with an enthusiastic team of staff.

Design

Depending on the VLE chosen, the amount of design which needs to be done will change (see also Chapter 7). Aspects which require designing include:

- **appearance;**
- **learning objects to be used;**
- **connection to the management information system (MIS);**
- **modifications to the VLE needed.**

The degree of modification to the VLE which users are allowed to carry out varies, with open-source systems allowing users a free rein. Certain limitations still apply, but these are normally concerned with distribution of any modifications. This may prove to be an important point if your school has specific requirements and the expertise to make changes. Open-source VLEs often have a raft of add-ons, such as blogging, which can be used to enhance the VLE and learning opportunities for your pupils. For example, you can link ELGG blogging software to Moodle (**http://elgg.net/**).

Many VLEs allow linking to the school's MIS so that pupil data, groupings, etc., may be used in the VLE. This may save a considerable amount of time in administrative tasks when assigning pupils to groups and providing usernames and passwords. It is worth investigating the VLEs supported by your MIS before deciding which VLE to use.

In addition to this, a detailed technical specification needs to be drawn up if it is to be a larger-scale project. This is likely to be handled by technical staff and should cover all technical steps which need to be taken in order to support the introduction of the VLE to meet its requirements.

Development

As with the design stage, the amount of development which needs to be done may range from none to a considerable amount, depending on the VLE chosen. The items which were specified in the design stage need developing. The development may be carried out by the school's own technical support, the VLE provider, or a third-party company.

If this is your own VLE set up by yourself, you will control the development.

Testing

The two stages of this section are testing of the technical specification from the design section, and testing of the requirement specification from the analysis section. It is likely that testing will be done on a small scale as the system has not yet been fully implemented.

During testing of the technical specification, technical staff test all the elements specified. Any elements which have not been fulfilled must either be remedied or a note made of the possible effects of not passing the test.

During testing of the requirement specification, the end users, i.e. staff and pupils, use the system and check that it meets all items listed in the requirements specification. Any short-comings identified at this stage need to be rectified before implementation.

PRACTICAL TASK PRACTICAL TASK **PRACTICAL TASK** PRACTICAL TASK **PRACTICAL TASK**

If you have access to a VLE that has been installed, create a course, then upload some work for your students. This might be a starter, discussed earlier in this book, or a piece of work that you already have in electronic format. If you don't have access to a VLE, but do have a computer/laptop, follow the instructions at the end of this chapter and download Moodle, then try uploading and using some work with one of your group.

This is probably the limit of the testing you will do if it is your own system you are installing and using.

Implementation

This is an often misunderstood word. In the context of the systems life cycle, it refers to the process of making the system 'live'. There are several standard methods of implementation, each of which makes it suitable under certain conditions.

- Direct implementation – in this case, the new VLE is rolled out to all staff and pupils. There is no duplication of tasks between the new VLE and any preceding systems. This method is usually used for projects in which a failure of the new system would not have disastrous effects on the users. As VLEs are complex pieces of software which often link to many other systems, it is unlikely that a failure would leave other systems unaffected. This makes direct implementation an unlikely candidate for implementing a VLE.
- Parallel implementation – both the new VLE and any preceding system are run side-by-side across the whole organisation. This ensures that any failure of the new system will not affect any other systems. While this is a 'safe' method of implementation, there are often increased support costs, as the new VLE as well as any previous systems would need to be technically supported. There is also the issue of teachers and pupils having to duplicate their efforts in some areas. This fact alone would make this method unsuitable, as time constraints are likely to prove an insurmountable problem.
- Phased implementation – in this method, different aspects of the VLE are introduced at different times. This has the effect of lessening the impact in terms of technical support and reducing the amount of new learning required by staff and pupils. Staff who are not particularly confident can more easily be supported using this method, and the decision to progress to the next phase can be delayed until all staff are competent and confident with the VLE.
- Piloted implementation – here, the VLE is tested initially with a small group of confident and competent users. These users would be more able to find errors in the system which would need addressing before rolling out to the rest of the staff. Such users would also be more likely to be keen early adopters of technology, and so more likely to find use for the VLE. As pilot users discuss the VLE with other members of staff, a positive attitude towards the VLE is being engendered, which makes rolling the system out to the rest of the staff easier.

After the choices of implementation method have been examined, it may well be decided that a combination of all four methods be used. For example, there may be some non-critical aspects of the VLE which are novel, and so they may by introduced through direct implementation. Other parts, for example, registration, are considered critical, and so would need the fallback of the old system to guard against problems. This would be likely to be introduced through parallel implementation. Other parts of the VLE could be introduced through a combination of piloted and phased implementation. For example, when it is decided to introduce audio summaries of topics, it may be best to introduce this one part to one department, initially. This department can then assess the ease of use, reliability and effectiveness before roll-out to the other departments.

A mixed mode of implementation would allow for the testing of the different parts of the VLE, and any faults reported and acted upon. It is important that the staff and pupils operate in an atmosphere where reporting faults is welcomed, and not seen as criticism.

When considering how to implement a VLE on a very small scale, it is advisable to install the VLE on a single computer and experiment with using different types of learning objects as suggested above. Other aspects of the VLE such as adding users and assigning users to teaching groups should be practised. Once you are confident with the basic use of the VLE, try installing it on a school server with access to the internet and allowing a small group of students access to the VLE. This constitutes a piloted implementation, as the system is being tested by a few users. It is also worth implementing the different learning objects one at a time so that time is allowed for you and the pupils to get used to their operation – phased implementation. Once use of the VLE has become established with the small group, use can then be widened to other groups, or members of staff as circumstances dictate.

A step-by-step guide to installing an open-source VLE is given at the end of this chapter.

Training and professional development in VLE use

A crucial part of implementation is training.

- Staff training – unless staff are trained adequately in advance of the introduction of the sections of a VLE, implementation is not likely to run smoothly. Ample time must be given to demonstrate the system to staff, allow staff to try the different aspects of the system and to ask questions. In order to support training, either printed or online training materials should be seriously considered. If these are not provided by the supplier of the VLE, then relevant materials can be produced fairly rapidly using screen capture software for printed or online support. It may be worth considering the option of paying the supplier or other training company to train staff, or asking your LEA for help with this. It is crucial that a supportive environment exists in order for staff who are unsure or experiencing difficulty to be able to ask questions or seek help.
- Pupil training – pupils tend to be much more eager to explore the potential of new technologies than staff as a whole, and so they should need less training on use of the system. They will need careful coaching, however, about the productive use of the system. Pupils must be made aware of exactly how the system aids their learning, and that while aspects such as forums and chat can be used for pleasure, excessive or inappropriate use is counterproductive.
- Pupils can also make the mistake of doing the same work electronically, rather than taking advantage of newer ways of working that a VLE offers. An example of this could be that pupils submit work electronically and review their feedback, resubmit work the next week, etc., without problems. They may not, however, have taken advantage of the rapid help they could get from teachers through forums or chat. They may not check their work for feedback regularly enough, or engage in the cycle of reviewing and resubmitting frequently enough.
- Support staff training – unless support for the VLE is going to be provided by an outside agency, the internal ICT support staff, if you have any, need to be made familiar with the system and its technical background. This task is much easier if the technical support staff have been involved with the information gathering, analysis, design and development phases. It may be the case that the support staff are already so familiar with the system that they just need pointing to places where support may lie, such as internet communities based around certain VLEs, technical support forums of suppliers' websites, etc.

Part of the implementation process in making the VLE useful to all curriculum areas is to enthuse staff from other areas so that they are more likely to take up the opportunities offered by the VLE. The key aspects of enthusing staff are to show the advantages to them of using the VLE and showing the advantages to students.

Benefits of VLE use to staff

In terms of benefits to staff, it is worth promoting the following aspects.

- Pupils will be able to access resources from home as well as school. Many staff already have a lot of resources available in electronic form. Any of these resources can be placed on the VLE. The VLE can also act as a central repository for resources, meaning that all staff in the department have access to all the resources at any time. This can prevent many of the problems involved in transferring work to and from school.
- Online assessments are a way of reducing teachers' workload. Once assessments are set up, they can be used for other groups, with the majority of VLEs providing some form of computerised

marking. VLEs usually allow summaries of assessments to be printed or exported for use in summative assessment and reporting to parents.

- There are several benefits of online assignments/projects. Any assignments can be marked at home or at school, again, without the problems of transferring/losing work. These assignments are available for work sampling and, in the case of course work, moderation. Staff also benefit from pupils having less opportunity to 'lose' work, as once it is uploaded, it can be accessed from any computer connected to the internet.
- Pupils are able to work collaboratively on projects, or peer-review each other's work. The benefits to the teacher are that there can be simple sharing of work, group evaluations and target setting, and the teacher can see which pupils have spent most time on the project.

Introducing the benefits of VLE use to pupils

Staff should see benefits to their pupils and their own teaching.

- Pupils can participate in 'anytime–anywhere learning'. This helps match learning patterns to pupils' preferred learning styles, and also allows curriculum access for pupils who, for whatever reason, are not attending school.
- There will be increased enthusiasm, as pupils are generally much more open to learning mediated by technology. This could lead to a higher proportion of deadlines being met, and a greater overall participation in the learning process.
- Pupils gain increasing independence, as VLEs provide a scaffold to enable pupils to engage in learning without direct supervision. Increased independence should result in greater performance, as the opportunities to achieve are much wider.
- Other benefits include faster feedback, linked target setting, chat forums, developing social skills, more 'fun' tasks, access to lesson materials that may have been missed due to absence, parents being able to share target setting, etc.

Maintenance

This stage should be the preserve of the ICT support staff, if you have them. It is important that boundaries are drawn, so that the support staff know exactly what their roles in the new system will be, e.g. backing up, updating, entering pupil information and liaising with suppliers. If this is done, and the support staff have received training, maintenance should run smoothly throughout the life of the system.

It is important that if there are support staff, their line manager is suitably briefed as to the important aspects of VLE maintenance so that routines and roles can be formalised and monitored. If the whole school is going to use the VLE, the system can be viewed as critical to the operation of the school, and maintenance procedures should be given a suitable priority.

If you are creating your own VLE you need to remember to take the usual steps such as protecting your computer with a virus checker, and ensuring that you regularly back up the system. This can be done simply using the facilities within the VLE itself.

Obsolescence

It is important that regular reviews of the VLE are held to assess whether it is still meeting all aspects of the requirement specification which was drawn up in the analysis section. When a departure from the requirements is found, it may be the case that a small modification may resolve the problem. This could be done either by in-house ICT support staff or by the supplier, depending on the system used. However, there may come a time when it is decided that the VLE is no longer fulfilling its requirements, or the requirements have changed so substantially that the VLE is of little use. At this stage the VLE has become obsolete and we return to the first stage to start the cycle again.

PRACTICAL TASK PRACTICAL TASK **PRACTICAL TASK** PRACTICAL TASK **PRACTICAL TASK**

Draw up a timeline for the implementation of your VLE. This should take into account all of the stages outlined above which are applicable to your particular situation. It may be useful to draw a Gantt chart to visualise all the stages. If you are not familiar with Gantt charts, an internet search will show you the basic layout. Such a chart is a great aid in a process which can be complex.

A final note

The preceding stages represent a logical series of actions which need to be carried out in order to introduce a VLE into a school. Even if you are only thinking of using a VLE for your own teaching, you need to go through many of the stages to some degree. However, when other teachers notice the effectiveness of the VLE, you may be pressured into widening the use of the VLE to the rest of the department, key stage or the school. In this case, as a key player in the project, the above stages are a good basis upon which to proceed.

RESEARCH SUMMARY RESEARCH SUMMARY **RESEARCH SUMMARY** RESEARCH SUMMARY

Ensminger et al (2004) found that the four main factors contributing to teachers accepting innovative new teaching methods were: good management of the change; them having the necessary skills, or being able to learn the necessary skills; receiving recognition for using the innovation; and having the resources to use the innovation.

Ebersole and Vorndam (2003) found that the major barriers to adoption of educational technology were lack of time, resources, confidence and perception of benefits. They also found that incentives proved to be 'being the right thing to do', personal satisfaction and student demand.

Stiles and Yorke (2003) found that when implementing new technologies, the pedagogical aspect was rarely given proper consideration, with support often being overlooked. They also found that in many cases, new technologies were introduced as a result of funding being available, rather than a need being demonstrated. The authors went on to describe a possible model of introduction.

CHAPTER **SUMMARY**

Before embarking on installing a VLE you need to consider carefully what your requirements and needs are.

You need to carry out a feasibility study that looks at the technical and economic aspects of the proposed VLE. Also, consider the social, legal, timescale and scale aspects of the VLE.

The next stage is to gather information relating to staff and pupil ability and confidence, technical support available, the technical aspects of your current system, and the teaching and learning styles of the staff and pupils who use it.

You then need to carry out an analysis relating to hardware, software and maintenance; consider the overall design, and potential development of the VLE.

Remember to consider the design, development and testing.

Carefully plan the implementation; focusing on the benefits to all those involved.

Finally, consider the maintenance and how soon the system needs updating/replacing.

You now have the knowledge to implement a small-scale VLE or work with a team to implement one across your school, or department.

What next?

You are now ready to set up a VLE, or start to upload your own teaching materials onto an existing VLE. If you are still very much at the learning stage and your only experience is as a user at university, then start to plan in small steps to upload teaching materials. Remember what we have said in this chapter about discussing with colleagues and your students to find out what they want, and how both you and they envisage using it. When you have uploaded some documents and used them in your lesson following advice contained earlier in this book, then remember to evaluate it. Our advice is to get it up and running as quickly as possible, while you are still enthusiastic. If you get stuck with any aspects, remember that most VLE supplier sites have chat forums so you can ask for help and advice. These usually have a great discussion area and opportunity to share materials. You will also find useful advice on the Becta website. Do enjoy using your VLE; it is a fantastic teaching and learning resource when used effectively.

Useful websites

insight.eun.org/ww/en/pub/insight/school_innovation/learnenv/archive/vle_checklist.htm – part of European Schoolnet, focusing on new technologies in education. This part of the site provides guidance on introducing a VLE.

www.becta.gov.uk – British Educational Communications and Technology Agency, contains a wealth of advice and research regarding implementing technology and hosting websites and VLEs.

www.moodle.com – hosting packages for the Moodle VLE.

elgg.net – producers of a variety of addition plugins for Moodle.

FURTHER READING FURTHER READING **FURTHER READING** FURTHER READING

Coppola, C and Neelley, E (2004) *Open source – opens learning: Why open source makes sense for education*. Arizona: r-smart group. Available at **www.rsmart.com/assets/OpenSource OpensLearningJuly2004.pdf**

Ebersole, S and Vorndam, M (2003) Adoption of computer based Instructional methodologies: A case study, *International Journal of e-Learning,* 2 (2), 15–20.

Ely, D (1999) Conditions that facilitate the implementation of educational technology innovations, *Educational Technology,* 39 (6), 23–27.

Ensminger, D C, Surry, D W, Porter, B E and Wright, D (2004) Factors contributing to the successful implementation of technology innovations, *Educational Technology and Society,* 7 (3), 61–72.

Gillespie, H (2006) *Unlocking learning and teaching with ICT*. London: David Fulton.

Newton, C and Tarrant, T (1992) *Managing change in schools: a practical handbook*. Abingdon: RoutledgeFalmer.

Stiles, M and Yorke, J (2003) Designing and implementing learning technology projects – a planned approach. Staffordshire University: EFFECTS/Embedding Learning Technologies Seminar, 8 April 2003.

Appendix – installing Moodle on a Windows machine

Step 1 – Download Easy PHP and Moodle

Easy PHP
Go to **http://www.easyphp.org/telechargements.php3** and click on the current version (at the top of the list)

Choose a location to download form and click the icon in the 'download' column.

Moodle
Go to **http://download.moodle.org** and download the 'latest stable branch' release in zip format.

Step 2 – Install Easy PHP
- This will install the PHP scripting language which Moodle uses, the MySQL database and the Apache web server.
- Double click on the Easy PHP file you downloaded.
- Select English as the language.
- Click Next.
- Accept the agreement and click next.
- Click on next.
- Click on next.
- Choose a location for the program; the standard one will probably suffice. Click on next.
- Choose a name for the entry on the start menu; again, the standard one will probably be fine. Click on next.
- Click on install.
- Click on finish.
- Click on Start, Programs, EasyPHP. This will start PHP, MySQL and the Apache web server.
- Once you see this screen with the traffic lights on green, you can minimise it.

Step 3 – Set up the MySQL database
- Open the settings for MySQL by right clicking on the 'e' icon, selecting 'configuration' and then 'PhpMyAdmin'. This is the admin tool for the MySQL database.
- Under the text 'Create a new database', enter the name 'moodle' and then click on create. This will create a database called moodle.
- Click on the home icon on the left.
- Click on 'privileges' to set the permissions for the database.
- To add a new database user, click on 'add a new user'.
- In the username box, enter 'moodle'.
- In the combo box under this, change it from 'use text field' to 'Any host'.
- Enter a suitable password in the 'password' and 're-type' boxes.
- Remember the username and password, as you will need them later.
- Click on check all, then on the go button at the bottom.
- You can then close this web page.

Step 4 – Install Moodle

- Unzip the Moodle files C:\Program Files\EasyPHP1-8\www This is the folder which the Apache web server stores the files it serves.
- Create an empty folder somewhere for Moodle to store its data. This should be called 'moodledata' and must not be in the www directory of EasyPHP.
- 'C:\Program Files\EasyPHP1-8\moodledata' would be a good idea.
- In a web browser, go to http://localhost/moodle (or wherever you unzipped the Moodle files to).
- You should now be in the setup system of Moodle. Click next to choose English.
- Click Next.
- Click Next.
- Enter the MySQL username and password you set up earlier.
- Click on next.
- Click on next.
- Moodle will now start setting the database up. You will be asked to click continue a number of times before getting to a configuration screen. Most of the settings can be left as standard.
- Click on 'continue' until you are asked to specify some site settings, the most important of which are the site name and the description of the site. The rest of the settings can be left as the defaults.
- Click on 'save changes' then on 'continue'.
- You will then be asked to specify a password for the admin user – do not forget or divulge this. You can then fill in other details about the admin user (you). You must include 'City/town', 'country' and 'description'.
- Click on 'update profile'.
- You will now be able to start Moodle by entering 'http://localhost/moodle' in the address bar of a web browser.

Further guidance can be found at **http://www.moodle.org**

Glossary

This glossary contains some of the words you may come across in this book or elsewhere in the context of virtual learning. Some can also be found in general educational contexts. The aim of this glossary is to define these terms specifically in the context of virtual learning.

Assignment An element of a VLE which allows teachers to set, assess and mark tasks done by learners. An assignment might be text- or image-based.

Asynchronous communication Communication where the participants do not take part at the same time. Examples include email and discussion boards.

Attendance A way of checking learners are present via the VLE. This tool may be linked to a school's management information system (MIS).

Blended learning A learning and teaching approach which combines traditional face-to-face teaching strategies and virtual learning strategies, which 'blend' together using the best elements of both.

Blog Short for 'weblog', a VLE or internet-based diary or record of ideas. Often used by people who are travelling to post photos and messages about their travels or by journalists as a record of events.

Broadband Fast internet access via DSL (digital subscriber line).

Calendar An element of a VLE which enables important dates and tasks to be shared between teachers and learners.

Chat room An internet or VLE-based area which allows teachers and learners to communicate synchronously by text. These are different from instant messaging forums as the user decides they wish to join the conversation rather than having to be invited.

Computer (PC or Mac) Computers are devices with microchips which allow the user to connect to the internet and create and use files of different types. They come in two main types, personal computers or PCs, which usually (although not always) run on a Microsoft Windows operating system. Apple Macs are only made by Apple and run on Mac Operating System (MacOS). Some computers run on an 'open source' or a UNIX operating system. Both of these types of computers are available in all sizes from small, handheld devices to large and powerful desktop computers. Almost all will now be able to connect to the internet via wireless or cables.

Dialogue A VLE communications tool which enables asynchronous communication between two learners and/or teachers.

Discussion board/forum An element of a website or VLE which allows synchronous and asynchronous communication between the uses of the forum. Messages can be posted and read and files can be exchanged.

Electronic portfolios (e-portfolios) Collections of electronic work which reflect a learner's engagement and achievement in a particular area of learning. These may contain a number of different files of different types, for example text files, presentations and video, which link together to form the whole portfolio.

Files area/digital drop box A place on a VLE where teachers and learners can keep and share files. Changing settings can enable different people to have different levels of access to the files.

Forum A VLE-based asynchronous discussion tool.

Glossary A VLE-based tool where teachers and learners can collect and define vocabulary linked to a particular subject or topic.

Gradebook A tool in a VLE which allows teachers and learners to view and use the results of online assessments.

Instant messaging A VLE or internet-based tool which allows two or more participants to have a synchronous text conversation and exchange files.

Internet The global network which links computers and allows them to communicate using a variety of protocols.

Learning object A name for a piece of content in a VLE, which could be a text file, a presentation or an image. Access to these can be controlled by the teacher.

Online A general term used to describe resources which are delivered using the internet, a VLE or learning platform.

Peer assessment Learners working together to review and assess one another's work. This is effectively done using a VLE where files can be shared.

Quiz An element of a VLE which enables teachers to set up assessments for learners. These might be informal or formal tests.

Survey An element of a VLE which enables teachers to survey, anonymously, learners' ideas and views.

Synchronous communication Communication where the participants take part at the same time.

Wikis Named after the first and best online editable encyclopaedia, Wikipedia. These internet or VLE-based tools allow teachers and learners to make and edit text files together in order to develop shared understandings of terms and definitions.

Workshop An element of a VLE which collects together resources and communications tools around a specific purpose.

World Wide Web A part of the internet. The prefix 'www' often appears at the beginning of web addresses or uniform resource locators (URLs).

Index

assessment 65–72
    case study 72
    and e-portfolios 68
    and learning objects 67–8
assignments 20, 68–9
    offline 22
    online 21
    text 21
    workshop 22
asynchronous tools 45–6
attendance monitoring 32–3

blended learning 7–18
    balance 15
    definitions 7, 18
    group/individual work 81
    ICT tools 82
    and main part of lesson 10–11
    online issues 16
    out of school 82
    parental involvement 13–14, 16–17, 69
    peer-to-peer assessment 11–12, 66
    plenary activities 14–15
    starter activities 8–10
    structure of lesson 81
    students' skills 82
    timing of lesson 81

calendar facility 24
case studies 5
chat rooms 33
choice facility 23
collaboration 41–2, 54
community formation 36–45
    asynchronous tools 45–6
    collaborative work 41–2
    critical mass 40
    pedagogical framework 36–7
    synchronous tools 43–5
    talk/chat/discussion 37–9
creativity 51–2

deadlines 20–1, 69
design issues 64–5, 75–83, 90–1
    blended learning 81–2
    look and feel 76
    organising content 80–1
    personalised learning 80–1
    primary users 77

    review of design 76–8
    secondary users 77–8
    text and images 79–80
    tools and communication 76
development 91
dialogue tool 32
discussion boards 44, 46

electronic portfolios 49–61
    advantages 51–5
    and assessment 67–8
    definition 49
    examples 50–1
    potential 60
    and primary phase 55–7, 59
    and secondary phase 57–8, 59
English as additional language 64

feasibility
    economic 86
    legal 87
    scalability 87
    social 86–7
    teaching/learning styles 89–90
    technical 85–6
feedback 70–1
forum facility 24–5

galleries 11
glossary 6, 99–100
    tool 26
gradebook 23
grading levels 68–9

homework 69

ICT (Information and Communications
    Technology) 1–2, 82
    staff confidence/student proficiency 88
implementation of system 91–4
inclusion 53
information
    analysis 90
    needs 88–9
instant messaging 34

learning objects 68–9, 76
learning platform *see* virtual learning
lesson 10–11

revision 11
structure/timing 81–2
tool 26–7
link
    to file 30–1
    to website 31–2

maintenance 94
managed learning environment *see* virtual
    learning
messaging, instant 34
Moodle installation 97–8
motivation 52
museums 11
'my files' area 33

National Curriculum 1–3
non-traditional school settings 63

obsolescence 94–5
online
    assignments 21
    issues 16
organising content 80–1
originality 55
out of school learning 82

parental involvement 13–14, 17, 69
pedagogical framework 37
peer-to-peer assessment 11–12, 66
personalised learning 81
plagiarism 55
plenary activities 14–15
portfolios *see* electronic portfolios
primary users
    design issues 77
    e-portfolios 55–6, 59
    text and images 79–80
professional development 3–4, 93
    and blended learning 8

QTS (Qualified Teacher Status),
    standards 5
quiz facility 27–8

reflective diaries 66
research summary 6
revision 11, 69
revision lessons 11

scalability 87
search engines 8–9

secondary users
    design issues 77–8
    e-portfolios 57–8, 59
    text and images 80
set up needs 84–96
    design *see* design issues
    development 91
    feasibility *see* feasibility
    ICT confidence/proficiency 88
    identification 84–5
    implementation 91–4
    information 88–90
        analysis 90
    maintenance 94
    obsolescence 94–5
    technical support 88
    technical system 88–9
    testing 91
    training 93
structure of lesson 81
students' skills 82
synchronous tools 43–5
systems *see* set up needs

target setting 70–1
tasks 5, 62–5
technical support 88
technical system 88–9
testing
    set up 91
    students 65–72
text assignments 21
text page 29
timing of lesson 81
training 9–12

value-added grading 68
virtual learning
    benefits to staff/students 93–4
    definition 1
    and National Curriculum 1–3
    objects 20–34, 68–9, 76
    and professional development 34, 91–2
    and schools 3
    and variety 66–7
VLE (Virtual Learning Environment) *see*
    virtual learning
voting and display 23

web page 28–30
website, link to 31
workshop assignment 22